Wales defeated England...

LYNN DAVIES

I would like to thank the staff at Y Lolfa for their co-operation in the publication of this book and in particular Eirian Jones for her much valued editorial guidance and assistance.

First impression: 2015

The publishers wish to acknowledge the support of Cyngor Llyfrau Cymru

Cover design: Y Lolfa

ISBN: 978 1 78461 116 3

Published and printed in Wales
on paper from well-maintained forests by
Y Lolfa Cyf., Talybont, Ceredigion SY24 5HE
website www.ylolfa.com
e-mail ylolfa@ylolfa.com
tel 01970 832 304
fax 832 782

In grateful memory of the late Kevin Thomas, of Ysbyty Gwynedd, Bangor, a particularly caring, inspirational consultant and fellow rugby fan.

Introduction

'Wales Defeated England...'

(Also a line from Max Boyce's 'Hymns and Arias'... which customarily elicits delirious applause.)

Some years ago, en route from the Twickenham rugby stadium to the local train station, a friend and I called at a nearby pub to seek temporary solace following a particularly unpalatable Welsh defeat at the hands of the English. As we desperately sought, over our pint glasses, to obtain some comfort from the proceedings of a disappointing afternoon, we attempted to garner a little justification for our misfortune by underlining the fact that the referee had performed rather badly, generally at the expense of Welsh interests. We were overheard by a home-team supporter sitting at the next table who took offence at our unwillingness to concede that we had been well beaten by a 'superior' team. A rather heated argument ensued which culminated in our English friend, with some disgust, bellowing 'Typical! You Welsh can't bloody take it when you lose,' at which point he returned to mingle with his friends, but not before we had vehemently invited him to withdraw from our company! Throughout this exchange a young man sitting between our table and that of our interloper had been smiling incessantly. When the above mentioned exchange of views had terminated he nudged me and asked, in a marked Australian accent, 'You mean, you hate the Poms as well?' To which I replied 'Yes, when they beat us at rugby!'

For losing to England has much wider repercussions than appearing to illustrate an apparent lack of rugby prowess. Such an occurrence can have a significant bearing on the *psyche* of the Welsh nation for a considerable time, in that the country consequently seems to be burdened by a *malaise* for which there seems to be a deeper explanation than that afforded by pure disappointment resulting from coming second-best in a rugby match. The 'Phil Bennett philosophy', as allegedly expounded by him in his captain's address to the team before they once played England, would seem to encapsulate the importance to his country of not allowing such a disaster to happen:

> Look at what the English have done to Wales. They've taken our coal, our water, our steel. They buy our houses and they only live in them for a fortnight every twelve months. What have the bastards given us? Absolutely nothing. We've been exploited, raped, controlled and punished by the English and that's who we're playing this afternoon! Come on Gar [Gareth Edwards] look what they're doing to your fishing, buying up rights all over the place for fat directors with big wallets. Those are *your* rivers, Gareth, yours and mine, not theirs!

However the England camp has been known, prior to matches against Wales, to express similar sentiments of dislike, none more contentious than the following comments attributed to prop Keith Fairbrother in the national press on the morning of the fixture between the two countries at Twickenham in 1970:

> I hate those bad-losing Welsh. I respect the Welsh for their playing ability and hardness. But I HATE them and can't stand to lose against them. Welshmen are bad losers. If they win they gloat. If they lose they moan. I don't think we rub it in enough when we win.

The Welsh coach at the time, Clive Rowlands, when he pinned those derogatory comments on the dressing room wall before the kick-off, needed no greater incentive to inspire his team to another Wales victory!

Yet in the eyes of many rugby-playing countries Fairbrother's remarks would seem to bring to mind the words 'pot', 'kettle' and 'black', particularly in the case of one celebrated 'Black', the renowned Grant Fox, who won 46 caps at outside-half for New Zealand. For him:

> ... of all the teams in the world you don't want to lose to England is top of the list. If you beat them, it's because you cheat. If they beat you, they've overcome your cheating!

It is no wonder, therefore, that to beat the English at rugby (one of the few sports at which we can consider ourselves superior to them!) is of paramount importance to the people of Wales. So, if losing to our neighbours can lead to a state of national depression, similarly being victorious against them is not only a source of unbridled pride and joy but serves also as a psychological boost to our national well-being.

Wales Defeated England... endeavours to describe the 56 Welsh victories, since our first encounter with England in 1881 up to the advent of the 2015 World Cup, and to capture the significance of each of those occasions. In so doing it is hoped that such a celebration of the past achievements of our country's rugby team might serve as an inspiration for further success.

1

15 February 1890: Dewsbury

1–0: Wales won by 1 try to nil.

In previous years kicking any kind of goal had been the all-important way of scoring points in rugby and a single goal was worth three tries. A goal was awarded for a successful conversion after a try, for a dropped goal or for a goal from a mark. If two teams were level following the goal count, or following a scoreless game, any unconverted try was taken into consideration to determine a winner. In 1890 a try was worth one point, which was increased to two points the following season, and to three points in 1893–4. Thus it remained until 1971–2 when a try became worth four points.

Wales: W.J. Bancroft (Swansea); D.P. Lloyd (Llanelli), +A.J. Gould (Newport), R.M. Garret (Penarth), D. Gwynn (Swansea); C.J. Thomas (Newport), W.H. Stadden; W.E.O. Williams, A.F. Bland, D.W. Evans (Cardiff), J. Hannan (Newport), W.H. Thomas (London Welsh), S. Thomas, (Llanelli), W.A. Bowen, J. Meredith (Swansea).

England: W.G. Mitchell (Richmond); P.H. Morrison (Cambridge Univ.), +A.E. Stoddart (Blackheath), J. Valentine (Swinton); J. Wright (Bradford), F.H. Fox (Malborough Nomads); A. Robinson, P.F. Hancock, F. Evershed, R.T.D. Budworth (Blackheath), J.H. Dewhurst (Richmond), S.M.J. Woods (Wellington), J.H. Rogers (Moseley), J.L. Hickson (Bradford), F. Lowrie (Batley).

+ denotes captain

The very first game between England and Wales had been played at Richardson's Field in Blackheath on 19 February 1881. The Welsh team had been selected by Richard Mullock, a Newport businessman, who had become a prominent sporting administrator in south Wales. The outcome of that first international between the two countries was a resounding victory for the home team, which, had the current points-scoring system been in operation, would have meant a scoreline of 82–0.

From the Welsh standpoint the whole event smacked of being a shambles. For example, England crossed for 13 tries, two of the selected Wales players didn't turn up and ten members of the team never played for their country again. However the debacle no doubt spurred the rugby fraternity in Wales to become better organised and to establish, some three weeks later, the Welsh Football Union (which then became the WRU), with Richard Mullock as its first Secretary.

Yet despite a number of encouraging performances during the following years, and victories against Ireland, Scotland and the New Zealand Maoris, Wales did not record her first victory against England until 1890, on the occasion of the seventh meeting between the two teams. England had been excluded from the home nations' championship in 1888 and 1889 following a disagreement with Scotland over a disputed try scored by the home team at Blackheath during the 1884 fixture between the two teams. The incident had led to the formation, by the three other home Unions, of the International Rugby Board (IRB) in 1887, the body which they deemed to be the new law-makers of the game.

Law-making duties had previously been assumed by England who objected to establishing the IRB and refused to join. The other three countries therefore banned them from playing in the home international championship until they agreed to join the IRB in 1890.

On their return to 'the fold', as it were, with a game against Wales in 1890, England once again became involved in a contentious scoring issue. However, this time Wales were deemed to be the transgressors, as a result of a try by W.H. 'Buller' Stadden, playing at half-back. He was registered as a Cardiff player but, by this time, enticed by the offer of generous expenses, he had joined Dewsbury (before the northern clubs had separated from the English Union) and had become a butcher in the town.

At the beginning of the second half 'Buller' made as if to throw the ball long at a line-out, deep in the England half. He was known as an expert at that tactic and the forwards accordingly backed away from the touchline as he prepared to throw. However, he suddenly bounced the ball infield, gathered it himself and crossed the English line for a try. His deception incurred the wrath of the visiting team but as the score was deemed to be within the parameters of the laws of the game at the time the try was allowed to stand. Sixteen years later such a tactic was banned by the rugby authorities!

Yet there was no doubt that Wales were the superior team in a match, played in front of 5,000 spectators, which saw their short, crisp passing game outshine the laborious efforts of the English backs to move the ball with long passes that often came to grief in the heavy, wintry conditions. In addition, resolute tackling and a magnificent kicking display from the 5' 5" Wales full-back, W.J. Bancroft, ensured that all English attacks were thwarted. Indeed the result served as an important justification of the attacking style of the visitors' play, implicit in their decision to employ four three-quarters, as opposed to England's three. As a result Wales had to compromise elsewhere and so opted to play just eight forwards against the nine-man England pack.

The Welsh practice of playing four three-quarters would, in due course, be copied by other nations to become the norm world-wide and recognised as a significant contribution to a more exciting style of play. The system had been pioneered by Cardiff Rugby Club, more by chance than by design. In 1884, F.E. Hancock appeared for the club as a replacement for one of the three regular three-quarters in a game against Cheltenham and scored two tries. Being loathe to drop him for the next game they decided to select four three-quarters, instead of three, and immediately reaped the benefits of the new style of play. During the following season they lost just one game, scoring 131 tries and yielding only four. However, against Scotland in 1886, a disappointing performance saw the four-man three-quarter system being abandoned by Wales for a few seasons until its reintroduction in 1889.

'Buller' Stadden never played for Wales again after that first victory against England. In due course he became a publican in Dewsbury and during Christmas Night in 1906 he strangled his wife in her bed, as his five children and a lodger slept close by. 'Buller' slashed his own throat with a knife and died three days later, at the age of 45 years.

2

7 January 1893: Arms Park, Cardiff

12–11: Wales won by 3 tries, 1 conversion and 1 penalty goal to 4 tries and 1 conversion

Wales: W.J. Bancroft (Swansea); N. Biggs (Cardiff), +A.J. Gould (Newport), J. Conway Rees (Llanelli), W. McCutcheon (Swansea); H.P. Phillips, F.C. Parfitt (Newport); T.C. Graham, J. Hannan, W.H. Watts, H.T. Day, A.W. Boucher (Newport), A.F. Hill (Cardiff), C.B. Nicholl (Llanelli), F. Mills (Swansea).

England: E. Field (Cambridge Univ.); R.E. Lockwood (Dewsbury), F.H.R. Alderson (Hartlepool Rovers), +A.E. Stoddart; H. Marshall, R.F.C. de Winton (Blackheath); J.H. Greenwell (Rockcliff), W.E. Bromet (Richmond), H. Bradshaw (Bramley), T. Broadley (Bingley), J.T. Toothill (Bradford), F. Evershed (Blackheath), S.M.J. Woods (Wellington), P. Maud, F.C. Lohden (Blackheath).

A remarkable game for many reasons, none more amazing than the fact that, owing to certain anomalies in the scoring systems being adopted at the time, many of the 15,000 spectators left the ground believing that Wales had snatched a draw, whereas in fact they had won the match. Two days before the game the IRB had met to confirm that the scoring system which would henceforth be applied to international matches was 2 points for a try (which was changed to 3 points the following season), 3 points for a conversion and a penalty goal, and 4 points for a drop goal. However, up until that time the WRU had been applying a system at club level of awarding 3 points for a try, 2 points for a conversion and 3 points for a penalty goal. Many of the spectators at the match that afternoon believed that the latter system was in operation, which would therefore have given a final score of 14–14, whereas the IRB's declaration two days previously meant that in fact Wales were the victors by 12–11.

It was also remarkable that the game had been played at all. Heavy frost and snow meant that on the day before, despite the fact that tons of straw had been put down earlier in the week, the pitch was frozen solid and it seemed likely that the match would have to be cancelled. However on the instigation of Bill Shepherd, a member of the Cardiff club committee, hundreds of portable street-watchmen fires, called 'devils', which devoured some 18 tons of coal, with boiler plates located underneath to spread the heat, burned at the ground throughout the night until 11 o'clock on the morning of the game. Such was the dramatic effect created by these measures that a visiting reporter from the *London Morning Leader* during that night likened the Arms Park to 'a scene from Dante's 'Inferno''.

The fare provided by both teams on the day indeed justified the efforts of the ground staff and numerous volunteers. The early exchanges were dominated by the nine-man England pack while their opponents, playing just eight forwards, were under constant pressure from their more physical counterparts. Tries by Lohden, after four minutes, then another by Marshall, converted by Stoddart, gave the visitors a deserved 7–0 lead at half-time.

Another Marshall try, following a decisive break from full-back Field and a telling foot-rush by his forwards, seemed to set the stage for an England victory. However, a brilliant try from centre Arthur Gould, who, capitalising on excellent work from forwards Nicholl and Hannan, dodged and darted his way to score underneath the posts following a magnificent run from halfway. With the wind now at their backs the Wales team, particularly the forwards, were galvanised to intensify their efforts. The England pack appeared to tire and, with 'Boomer' Nicholl haranguing his team in Welsh, another exciting Wales move by the four-man three-quarter line saw Conway Rees (who had to retire shortly afterwards having gamely tried to play on with a broken collarbone) put the Cardiff winger, Norman Biggs, away, with the English defence outnumbered, to make the score 7–9.

He was winning his fourth cap that day having first been chosen for his country four years earlier at the age of 18 years. He played for Cardiff for 22 consecutive seasons and represented Glamorgan at cricket. Five of his brothers also played rugby for Cardiff, with one of them, Selwyn, being capped nine times for Wales. Norman was a police officer in the Glamorgan Constabulary and, having fought as a soldier in the Boer War, eventually became a superintendent in the Nigerian Police Force. In 1908, at the age of 37 years, he was unfortunately killed by a poisoned arrow during a native insurrection in that country.

Following the Biggs try, and with the visitors' backs constantly on the defensive, England were forced to withdraw Sam Woods from the scrum for a time to play as a three-quarter. However, with their captain, Stoddart, intent on regaining forward superiority Woods was recalled and another inspired dribble by the pack led to Marshall going over for his third try. Stoddart failed to convert, which made the score 7–11 with ten minutes remaining.

This spurred Wales and their captain Gould to even greater efforts and a blistering, evasive run from him led to Wales scoring their third try. They were now within two points of the visitors' score, with the conversion, which could put Wales in the lead, to follow. Unfortunately, the usually reliable W.J. Bancroft of Swansea missed a comparatively easy kick. However, the aspirations of the despondent home supporters were dramatically revived when Wales were awarded a last-gasp penalty near the touchline on the England 25-yard line. It was anticipated that lining up such a kick would be a mere formality for Bancroft. He was one of the most senior and reliable players in the team. He had played in that first victory against England three years previously and Gould was the only member of the team who had played more games than him for Wales.

However, when he prepared to take that fateful last-ditch penalty to win that game for Wales in 1893, he became the subject of great controversy and of much debate following the game. There is no disputing the fact that from the penalty he opted to kick an excellent drop goal – the very first penalty goal to be scored in the Home Championship. However it was said that he did this against the wishes of his captain Arthur Gould, who, in a fierce discussion with him at the spot from where the kick would occur, wanted Bancroft to take a place-kick. Bancroft refused, explaining later that he went for the drop goal because the ground was too hard to make a decent platform for a place-kick.

It is said that the fact that Gould threw the ball at Bancroft's feet, as opposed to handing it to him, was indicative of his annoyance at having his instructions ignored. As indeed was his decision to stand on the halfway line and turn his back on the kick, some say in disgust, while others claimed that he did so because its importance meant that he was too nervous to watch it. Nevertheless he was soon appeased when he heard Bancroft's joyous shout 'It's there Arthur!'

Within minutes Wales had become winners of the Triple Crown and the Championship. Former *Western Mail* sports editor John Billot quotes a local rugby correspondent's description of the scene:

> Thousands streamed down from the stands and poured towards the exits in two great cheering mobs. The players were borne away to the Angel Hotel, shoulder high and the sight and sound of enthusiasm was something to remember. The victory simply sent the population of Cardiff, plus the thousands of visitors, off their blessed chumps. It will take some of us at least a week to get over it.

3

9 January 1897: Rodney Parade, Newport

11–0: Wales won by 3 tries and 1 conversion to nil

Wales: W.J. Bancroft (Swansea); C. Bowen (Llanelli), E.G. Nicholls (Cardiff), +A.J. Gould, T.W. Pearson (Newport); S. Biggs (Cardiff), D. Jones (Aberavon); H. Packer, A.W. Boucher (Newport), W. Morris, J. Evans (Llanelli), R. Hellings (Llwynypia), F. H. Cornish (Cardiff), D. Evans, J. Rhapps (Penygraig).

England: J.F. Byrne (Moseley); E.F. Fookes (Sowerby Bridge), E.M. Baker (Oxford Univ.), F.A. Byrne (Moseley), T. Fletcher (Seaton), C.M. Wells (Harlequins), +E.W. Taylor (Rockcliff), F. Jacob (Cambridge Univ.), J.H. Barron (Bingley), P.J. Ebdon (Wellington), R.F. Oakes (Hartlepool Rovers), W.B. Stoddart (Liverpool), F.M. Stout (Gloucester), W. Ashford, R.H. Mangles (Richmond).

This was a particularly welcome victory in view of the fact that Wales hadn't beaten England since 1893 and had surprisingly been thrashed 25–0, yielding seven tries, in the corresponding fixture the previous year. As a result of the win Wales were undefeated at the end of the season, as this was the only game they had played in the Home Nations Championship! Shortly after the England match the WRU had withdrawn from the IRB owing to a dispute over the Welsh captain, the 32-year-old Newport centre, Arthur Gould, who had come out of retirement to play for his country for the 27th and last time and in front of his home crowd.

'Monkey' Gould (apparently so-called because of his agility as a child when climbing trees) was the first 'pin-up' boy of Welsh rugby. His natural style was the epitome of 'the Welsh way' of playing the game and did much to enhance his country's

A.J. Gould skippers Wales for the last time

reputation in rugby circles. His speed was remarkable; indeed in 1892 he was the Midlands hurdles champion over 100 and 120 yards and in recent years had earned a considerable sum of money as a sprinter. Coupled with that attribute was his ability to produce a devastating swerve at speed and a telling, quicksilver sidestep. In the words of Gwyn Nicholls, his fellow centre, trying to stop Gould when he was in full flight was like 'trying to catch a butterfly with a hatpin'!

Such was the adulation that 'Monkey' attracted that his supporters in Newport, towards the end of his playing career, contributed to a testimonial fund set up in his name. The proceeds of the fund were used to present him, as a gift, with the deeds of a new, detached house in Newport, not long after the 1897 match against England. The occasion of the presentation, chaired by the WRU president, was itself an indication of the regard which the rugby public of Wales had for their captain. Two hundred and fifty people from amongst the great and the good of the nation attended a special dinner to honour him, with adjacent public galleries crammed with adoring spectators to witness the event.

The other home countries deemed Gould's reward to be a manifestation of professionalism in the amateur game of rugby union. Consequently, Ireland and Scotland refused to play Wales that season, leading to the latter's withdrawal from the IRB in protest and to national indignation at the perceived insult. However, after Gould had facilitated a reconciliation by declaring his irrevocable decision to retire as a player, Wales were readmitted to the IRB in 1898 and normal fixtures were resumed that year, albeit on a protracted date.

The 1897 game against England was played on a wet, wintry day in heavy conditions. Yet Wales had resisted the temptation to pick a bulky pack, as their opponents invariably were wont to do. Instead, they opted for rugged, more mobile forwards who, although they could hold their own in the tight, also possessed rugby skills that served them well in loose play. On the day four members of the pack played their club rugby for Rhondda teams (Jack Evans, although registered with Llanelli, at the time turned out regularly for Llwynypia) with the result that from that day the term 'Rhondda forward' was coined in rugby circles to depict a certain style of play as epitomised by those four players.

Indeed the Welsh pack were the masters of their English counterparts and the three Welsh tries, by Pearson, Boucher and Jones, were the result of prominent forward drives, as the conditions demanded. They were aided by the controlled kicking of Gwyn Nicholls and a sterling defensive performance from Gould. His final contribution to international rugby was to create scrum-half Jones's try with a deceptively delicate chip. It was generally agreed that Wales should have won by a far greater margin, such was their superiority on the day. Yet this was the first time that they had defeated England by more than one point.

Arthur Gould went on to referee and to serve as a selector for the national team. He had captained his country on 18 occasions in 27 appearances, which remained a record until 1994 when Ieuan Evans led Wales for the 19th time in a World

Cup qualifying match against Portugal. Gould's work as a public works contractor at times took him away from Newport which meant that during his career he also represented English clubs. At one stage his rugby career was interrupted when he took up employment for a time in the West Indies. He eventually became clerk of the works in his home town and was also employed as a brewery representative. He died in 1919 and was buried in Newport after what was described at the time as the biggest funeral ever held in Wales.

The 1897 match against England was Gwyn Nicholls's first appearance against England and his third in a Wales jersey. On Gould's retirement Nicholls took over his mantle as the star of the Wales team and as a result of his reputation as a brilliantly deceptive runner he became known by the title 'Prince of Three-quarters'. He was also a resolute defender but perhaps his greatest attribute was the manner in which he created time and space for other players outside him. Rhys Gabe, Nicholls's fellow centre, both with Cardiff and Wales, during the latter part of his career and who was invited to unveil the Gwyn Nicholls Memorial Gate at Cardiff Arms Park in 1949, described him as:

> ... the complete centre three-quarter. In attack he always
> ran straight as he lived and his abiding passion was to make
> things easy for his *confrères* to carry on – the very antithesis
> of selfishness... His own defence was impregnable – this the
> spectators saw, but what they did not see was his unfailing support
> for everyman in his side.

In 1899 Nicholls toured with the British Isles team to Australia, the only Welshman to be selected. He became the star of the team and returned home with a significantly enhanced reputation. In 1909 his final contribution to international rugby was to referee the match between England and Scotland, after which he declared, 'Wasn't I awful!'

4

7 January 1899: St Helen's, Swansea

26–3: Wales won by 6 tries and 1 conversion to 1 try

Wales: +W.J. Bancroft (Swansea); H.V.P. Huzzey, E.G. Nicholls (Cardiff), R.T. Skrimshire (Newport), W.M. Llewellyn (Llwynypia); E. James, D. James (Swansea); J. Blake, T. Dobson (Cardiff), W.H. Alexander (Llwynypia), F.G. Scrine (Swansea), D.J. Daniel (Llanelli), A. Brice (Aberavon), J.J. Hodges (Newport), W. Parker (Swansea).

England: H.T. Gamlin (Devonport Albion); R. Forrest (Wellington), P.W. Stout (Gloucester), P.M.R. Royds (Blackheath), G.C. Robinson (Percy Park); R.O'H. Livesay (Blackheath), +A. Rotherham; H.W. Dudgeon, F. Jacob, (Richmond), J. Daniell (Cambridge Univ.), C.H. Harper (Exeter), W. Mortimer (Malborough Nomads), G.R. Gibson (Northern), J. Davidson (Aspatria), R.F. Oakes (Hartlepool Rovers).

The English press before the game appeared to look forward to the formality of another victory for the visitors despite having to field seven new caps. Wales, too, had seven newcomers in their team, including the 20-year-old Willy Llewellyn, of the Llwynypia club, on the left wing. His debut could not have been more auspicious as he crossed for a record four tries, two in each half (the other two tries were scored by the right wing Huzzey, of Cardiff) whereas Robinson got the solitary England try. Llewellyn's first try came about when he charged down a clearance kick, gathered and darted over the line. His second followed good work on the blind side by the James brothers, while Parker put him away for his third after he himself had started the move from broken play. His final try resulted from a cross-kick by Bancroft.

The Welsh selectors had been rather slow to recognise his prowess, since during the previous season he had scored 50 tries for his club. He went on to gain a further 19 caps and was the subject of much adulation during his career. He was a pharmacist by profession and it is said that during the Tonypandy riots of 1910, when a great deal of damage was done to commercial properties, Willy Llewellyn's chemist shop was one of the few businesses to remain unscathed, such was the respect that he commanded.

Despite his stellar contribution to the victory, the greatest plaudits went to the two brothers from Swansea who played at half-back, Evan and David James. During that time the positions of inside- and outside-half were interchangeable during a game and both players were masters of either. They mesmerised their opponents and dazzled the 25,000 crowd, ably assisted on the day by the brilliance of W.J. Bancroft, Gwyn Nicholls and Llewellyn. Indeed Evan had broken his collarbone after just five minutes, but continued to pose a threat to his opponents for the remainder of the game.

Yet Wales, over the years, were prevented from utilising the talents of the James brothers in full. For David and Evan won just four and five caps respectively between 1890 and 1899. They were both labourers in the White Rock copper works in Swansea and having failed to get the Swansea club to pay them £1.10s. a week, they joined Broughton Rangers, one of the English rugby league clubs. As a result they were banned by the rugby union authorities but following an appeal by the WRU they were reinstated in 1896.

While playing for Swansea the diminutive brothers (Evan measured 5' 7½" and David 5' 6") had assumed legendary status. Known as 'the Swansea gems' and 'the curly-headed marmosets', the artistry and skills which they displayed on the field were often said to have an affinity with music hall entertainment. Their attributes became part of local folklore and tales of their accomplishments bordered on the unbelievable. Their reputation it seems had spread afar since the captain of an Ireland side, in his pre-match team talk before playing against Wales, had advised his players, when the James brothers came at them, 'to go for the one who hasn't got the ball, because he will be the one that has!'

Their obsession with perfection meant that they were constantly practising. It was said that, in the absence of a ball, rather strange substitutes would suffice, e.g. kettles, pots, pans, copper ladles, loaves of bread and even an undertaker's hat. It was even claimed that they sometimes resorted to practise their passing skills using a baby! Their efforts certainly bore fruit in that 1899 game against England.

The team had decided to gather for an unprecedented practice session at Cardiff Arms Park on the Wednesday before the game, so that they could become acquainted with each other's style of play. For example, the James brothers had never previously played with any of the Wales three-quarters. That decision certainly paid off in the match itself. For, despite the fact that the visitors had dominated the early play, the Wales backs, having been given a solid platform by their forwards, frequently ripped through the England defence with some breathtaking play.

English supporters and rugby reporters alike saw their defeat as a humiliation and recognised that whereas their style of play had seemed dated and ponderous, the Welsh approach was considerably more enlightened and exciting. Indeed there was no real improvement in England's fortune for some time to come, for this particular game turned out to be the first of 12 consecutive defeats against the men in red.

It was also the last appearance of the James brothers for their country, for they returned to play for Broughton soon afterwards, with 16 members of the family in all deciding to uproot to the north of England. Each of the brothers had been given a £200 signing on fee and promised a £2 a week match fee. However, their stay was short on that second occasion, for it is said that David's wife, a Welsh speaker from Bonymaen, found it hard to settle in Lancashire and suffered greatly from *hiraeth* for her family and her locality. Evan died from TB at the age of 30 and David resumed his work as a ladler in the copper works, although it is said that he had previously rejected an offer to become rugby coach at Mill Hill School, London.

5

6 January 1900: Kingsholm, Gloucester

13–3: Wales won by 2 tries, 2 conversions and 1 penalty goal to 1 try

Wales: +W.J. Bancroft (Swansea); W.M. Llewellyn (Llwynypia), D. Rees, G. Davies, W.J. Trew (Swansea); L.A. Phillips, G.Ll. Lloyd (Newport); R. Hellings (Llwynypia), A. Brice (Aberavon), W.H. Millar (Mountain Ash), W.H. Williams (Pontymister), B. Thomas (Swansea), G. Boots, J.J Hodges (Newport), J. Blake (Cardiff).

England: H.T. Gamlin (Devonport Albion); S.F. Cooper, G. Gordon-Smith (Blackheath), A. Brettargh (Liverpool O.B.), E.T. Nicholson (Birkenhead Park); +R.H.B. Cattell (Moseley), G.H. Marsden (Morley); F.J. Bell, R.W. Bell (Northern), W. Cobby (Hull), A. Cockerham (Bradford Olicana), J.W. Jarman (Bristol), S. Reynolds (Richmond), C.T. Scott (Blackheath), J. Baxter (Birkenhead Park).

The Wales team had been announced on 15 December and included the incumbent centre, Gwyn Nicholls, one of the new stars of Welsh rugby who would have been winning his ninth cap. However, having toured with the British Isles team to Australia during the previous summer, he had gone missing. Rumour had it that he had enlisted to fight against the Boers in South Africa and his disappearance remained a mystery until the end of December when his father revealed that he had received a telegram from his son stating that he would not be home in time for the England match. In due course Nicholls arrived back at Cardiff station on 13 January, where he was welcomed by a large crowd.

Until England settled for Twickenham as their permanent home in 1910, the country's individual clubs applied to their union to host their home internationals. The Gloucester club however must have regretted its decision to extend an invitation to hold this match against Wales for a number of reasons. Firstly, the event incurred a significant financial loss of some £700 for the Kingsholm club. This was attributed to the fact that, although around 15,000 attended, advance ticket sales were disappointing, due partly to the fact that no local players had been selected and that the anticipated numbers of travelling Wales supporters did not materialise.

In addition, a major disaster was narrowly avoided when part of the 'shilling enclosure' in the ground collapsed an hour before the kick-off, with some 200 spectators being thrown to the ground. The construction of the stand had been temporarily secured with nails, with the intention of replacing them later with the required bolts. Unfortunately, the worker responsible was taken ill before that task could be undertaken. Surprisingly, no serious injuries were reported.

The game was both fast and furious. The Welsh half-backs, capitalising on an excellent supply of ball from the lighter Welsh forwards, outshone their disappointing English counterparts. The sparkling play of the Welsh three-quarters, despite the fact that a number of their attacking ploys failed to come to fruition, was far superior to that of the visitors, who suffered from a distinct lack of understanding when attempting passing movements. This perhaps reflected the fact that few of the team, which included 13 new caps, had played together before. This remained a record for the Championship until 1947, when the resumption of fixtures, after an eight-year gap because of the Second World War, saw France, Scotland and England select a greater number of newcomers.

Yet England managed to stay in contention for much of the match and Wales led by just 5–0 at the interval, as a result of a try by Hellings. A period of sustained forward pressure in the home team's 25 saw the pack surge for the line with the Llwynypia forward eventually carrying over to touch down. Bancroft kicked the conversion but Hellings had fractured his forearm in scoring and played on in great pain for the rest of the game with his arm hanging limply by his side.

With both defences being severely tested early in the second half, England broke the deadlock when winger Nicholson crossed for a try in the corner, following a fine run by scrum-half Marsden, which Gamlin failed to convert. Brilliant handling by the Welsh backs saw the visitors reply with a try behind the posts from the 20-year-old Swansea winger Billy Trew, playing in his first game for Wales. His debut saw the birth of one of the most illustrious Welsh international careers. He was described by Rhys Gabe, a contemporary of Trew's in the Wales back line for much of his career, as 'the most complete footballer who ever played for Wales'. He went on to play another 28 games for his country in an international career that lasted until 1913, when he was 33 years old.

A boilermaker by trade, who later became a publican, he sometimes courted controversy. For example, he refused to play against Ireland in 1907 in protest against the suspension of his Swansea club-mate, Fred Scrine, by the WRU, for 'using improper language to a referee'. As a result, Wales took the field in that game without a single Swansea player in the team for the first time since 1882. Again Trew, because of injury, was not selected for the 1912 match against England at Twickenham. He had watched the game from the stand and was later arrested in the Strand for being drunk and disorderly.

His delicate, somewhat sickly appearance, which his slender build of 5' 8" and 10 stone 9lbs seemed to accentuate, belied a tough, uncompromising attitude. Despite being regularly targeted for rough treatment by opponents, resulting in many injuries, his dedication was always unflinching. He was a natural athlete who was seen at times to jump bodily over potential tacklers. Yet his trademark was a drifting, ghost-like running style, deceptively accomplished at speed, coupled with a devastating swerve. His talent in that respect was often utilised to create space for others and was indicative of the excellent tactical awareness that he possessed. That is further illustrated by the fact that he captained his country on 14 occasions (with 12 of those games resulting in Welsh victories) and, after playing on the wing in his first six international matches, was from then on selected at centre or outside-half.

The final score in that game against England in 1900 was a penalty goal by Bancroft, giving Wales victory by 13–3, which in the opinion of some critics flattered the home team. Yet there was no denying that the Wales backs, having been given a considerable supply of possession by the forwards, had shown indications of exciting and rewarding times to come. Indeed the game marked the beginning of the first Welsh 'Golden Era', which saw the team winning, during a 12-year period, six Championships and six Triple Crowns and suffering just six defeats and never finishing below second place in the Championship table. During that time they scored 132 tries at an average of 11 tries per season, with the 1910–11 period proving to be exceptional, when Wales scored, in the eight matches played, a total of 166 points and 39 tries. By comparison, during those 12 years England won only one Championship and were left with the Wooden Spoon on five occasions.

Billy Trew retired from playing rugby at club and international level in 1913, and later became a national selector. He died at the comparatively young age of 46 years, with crowds lining the streets of Swansea to pay their last respects on the occasion of his funeral. His premature passing, in the opinion of some, was a result of the many batterings he took on the rugby field. There was one particularly amusing postscript to the 1900 encounter. The England captain and outside-half, the Revd R.H.B. Cattell, was reported to have made an official complaint that one of the Wales forwards, during the match, had called him 'a pig'!

6

5 January 1901: Arms Park, Cardiff

13–0: Wales won by 3 tries and 2 conversions to nil

Wales: +W.J. Bancroft (Swansea); W.M. Llewellyn (Llwynypia), E.G. Nicholls (Cardiff), G. Davies, W.J. Trew (Swansea); G.Ll. Lloyd (Newport), J. 'Bala' Jones (Aberavon); R. Hellings (Llwynypia), A. Brice (Aberavon), W.H. Millar (Mountain Ash), G. Boots, J.J. Hodges (Newport), J. Blake (Cardiff), R. Thomas (Swansea), W.H. Williams (Pontymister).

England: J.W. Sagar (Cambridge Univ.); E.W. Elliot (Sunderland), +J.T. Taylor (Castleford), E.J. Vivyan (Devonport Albion), C. Smith (Gloucester), E.J. Walton (Castleford), R.O. Schwarz (Richmond); H. Alexander (Birkenhead Park), A.F.C. Luxmoore (Richmond), C.T. Scott (Blackheath), N.C. Fletcher (OMT), D. Graham (Aspatria), C.O.P. Gibson (Northern), E.W. Roberts (RNC Dartmouth), A. O'Neill (Torquay).

Perhaps the most notable aspect of this disappointing game was the manner in which the Wales scrum-half, John 'Bala' Jones, earned his only cap for his country. On the morning of the match he had been enjoying a drink in the Queen's Hotel when the selected scrum-half, Lou Phillips (Newport), informed the Welsh selectors that he didn't feel well enough to play. As a result 'Bala' Jones, who played for Aberavon at the time, was asked to turn out in Phillips's place. His selection was all the more remarkable due to his having been designated as a professional by the WRU three years previously on the occasion of his joining the Devonport Albion club, only to be later reinstated as an amateur when he appealed against that decision.

One of the surprising aspects of the Wales performance on this day was that full-back Bancroft played so badly, which he attributed to the fact that a thigh strain had prevented him from training properly. However, he also disappointed in the two remaining international matches that season with the result that the game against Ireland on 16 March 1901 was his last in the red jersey. In all he played in 33 consecutive matches for Wales (a record which stood until broken by Ken Jones in 1955) over 12 seasons. No full-back played more games for Wales until J.P.R. Williams, against Scotland in 1977, appeared for his country for the 34th time.

In 1898 he had become the team's captain on the occasion of his 23rd cap. He was a prodigious kicker, from the hand and from the ground with either foot, and during his time with Wales he took every penalty that the team were awarded. Perhaps it is an indication of his skill and dedication that during team practices he would regularly succeed in kicking the ball between the posts from the corner flag.

But he was also renowned for his sparkling, sidestepping runs, despite his diminutive 5' 5½" build. He would frequently delight in throwing the ball to himself from line-outs and embark on ambitious runs, even from his own goal-line, with the result that he was sometimes accused of playing to the gallery. He sometimes suffered because of his lack of physicality, for example in a game in 1899 he was engulfed by Micky and John Ryan, two brothers playing in the Irish pack, and thrown into the crowd! He was forced to retire to the changing rooms with two broken ribs.

As a child he was brought up at the St Helen's ground in Swansea where his father and grandfather before him were groundsmen. Although a cobbler by trade, W.J. later followed in the family tradition and became a groundsman there too. He was also an excellent cricketer, playing as an opening batsman and wicketkeeper for Glamorgan. Indeed in 1895 when he was 24 years old, he became the first professional cricketer to play for the county (they did not achieve first-class status until 1921) when he obtained a contract for 20 weeks at a wage of £2 a week.

As a cricketer he could lay claim to many notable

The Wales team led by W.J. Bancroft

achievements. Between 1889 and 1914 he scored seven centuries and accumulated 8,353 runs. He scored a half-century against South Africa in 1901 and also played for Glamorgan against Australia in 1902. Despite his own success as a player, he would claim that his proudest sporting achievement was to see his protégé, Gilbert Parkhouse, play cricket for England.

In the rugby match in question against England he frequently failed to find touch with his clearances with the result that Wales were often under pressure. They suffered further from a distinct lack of effort and urgency from their pack, yet they were still far too good for the visitors. They took the lead as a result of a first half try from Jehoida Rogers (Newport), one of the most versatile Welsh forwards ever, with Bancroft kicking the first of his two conversions in the match. Rogers played for his country on 23 occasions between 1899 and 1906 and was one of the stalwarts of the 1905 victory against the All Blacks.

Wales went further ahead in the second half when centre Gwyn Nicholls used his powerful 6 feet and 11 stone 6lbs frame to break past his marker with a decisive hand-off and crash over the line with a number of English defenders on his back. Another try by the Pontymister forward, W.H. 'Buller' Williams secured the victory, yet, despite a rousing finale, the general opinion was that it had been one of the most disappointing of Welsh winning performances.

7

11 January 1902: Blackheath

9–8: Wales won by 2 tries and 1 penalty goal to 2 tries and 1 conversion

Wales: J. Strand Jones (Llanelli); W.M. Llewellyn (Llwynypia), +E.G. Nicholls (Newport), R.T. Gabe (Llanelli), E. Morgan (London Welsh); R. Jones, R.M. Owen (Swansea); A. Brice (Aberavon), J.J. Hodges, G. Boots (Newport), W. Joseph (Swansea), D. Jones (Treherbert), W.T. Osborne (Mountain Ash), A.F. Harding (Cardiff), N. 'Danny' Walters (Newport).

England: H.T. Gamlin (Devonport Albion); P.L. Nicholas (Exeter), J.E. Raphael (OMT), J.T. Taylor (Castleford), S.F. Cooper (Blackheath); P.D. Kendall (Birkenhead Park), B. Oughtred (Hartlepool Rovers); +H. Alexander (Birkenhead Park), D.D. Dobson (Newton Abbot), L.R. Tosswill (Exeter), S.G. Williams (Devonport Albion), T.H. Willcox (Plymouth), J. Jewitt (Hartlepool Rovers), G. Fraser (Richmond), J.J. Robinson (Headingley).

Wales were captained for the first time by Gwyn Nicholls, who had served his apprenticeship as a successful skipper of Cardiff and was making his 14th appearance for his country. At this time he was playing for Newport, since he and his brother-in-law, the Welsh international full-back, Bert Winfield, had moved to the town to become part of a family laundry business. However, later that season he returned to Cardiff where he and Winfield set up their own business which became the most successful laundry company in south Wales.

The occasion at Blackheath provided a particularly Welsh atmosphere. Large numbers of supporters had travelled there from Wales and it was claimed that en route to the Rectory Field more Welsh was spoken than English. In addition the visitors made their presence felt with rousing renditions of favourites such as 'Sospan Fach', much to the amazement of watching English supporters and residents. The travelling supporters were doubtless a great inspiration for the Welsh team which contained seven new caps.

Among the forwards who were wearing the red jersey for the first time was the 20-year-old coal miner, Dai 'Tarw' Jones. He was renowned for his physical prowess and, at 6' 1" and weighing 15 stone 4lbs, was bigger than most other forwards at that time. He won 13 caps in all and later had the distinction of playing in two victories against New Zealand, firstly with Wales against the All Blacks in 1905 and then, in 1908, against the All Golds, when he appeared for the Wales rugby league side at Aberdare before 17,000 spectators. He had moved to play rugby league when he and a number of others had been banned by the WRU for accepting payment for playing. He later joined the police force but, having physically and aggressively removed an inspector from Treherbert Police Station who had apparently annoyed him, he returned to being a collier!

Apart from Gwyn Nicholls and Willy Llewellyn, the remaining five backs in the game in question had only three previous caps between them. Yet Wales opened the scoring with an excellent try from centre Rhys Gabe, playing for his country for only the second time, after good work by Strand-Jones. The Llanelli full-back had narrowly earned selection over Bert Winfield to win his first cap, in place of W.J. Bancroft, to whom he was often compared due to a similar style of play. He was a former Theology student at Saint David's College, Lampeter, and at Oxford before being appointed eventually as a chaplain in Lahore.

In engineering that first try at Blackheath he had broken from a defensive position and, instead of kicking for touch, rounded the English forwards, sidestepped Cooper, the opposing left-wing, and passed to Gabe some 25 yards from the try line. The Welsh winger, according to *Fields of Praise*:

... had only to round Gamlin, the full-back. He did so at the cost of a blow to his solar plexus from an outstretched arm, stumbled on, scored and passed out. Gamlin, over 6 foot and 14 stone, was compared variously to an octopus and to a boa-constrictor; he did not so much tackle a man as crush him. If his deadly tackles were evaded there were still arms which seemed to reach out after he had been passed to do the necessary evil.

It was indeed quite an achievement to floor Rhys Gabe in such a manner, for he was a tough, crash-tackling centre who measured 5' 11" and weighed 12 stone 9lbs. He was renowned for his hard, straight running, yet could leave opponents flummoxed by a rapid change of direction when required. Having attended Borough Road Training College he became a schoolteacher in Cardiff in 1903, whereupon he joined the Cardiff club. He was an all-round sportsman who played cricket for Glamorgan and captained Radyr Golf Club.

The Welsh lead was short-lived, for England hit back with two tries from their forwards Dobson and Robinson, the first of which was scored under the posts and was duly converted, thus putting the home team ahead at half-time by 8–3. Wales retaliated in the second half when flanker W.H. Osborne crossed for a try to make the score 8–6, which remained so until five minutes from the end of the game, when a crafty piece of deception by Dicky Owen paved the way for the Welsh victory.

The Swansea scrum-half, hovering at the base of the scrum following a Welsh heel, and urging his forwards in Welsh not to release the ball, feigned to pick up, thus enticing the opposing scrum-half, Bernard Oughtred, to make a tackle in an off-side position, near the posts. (His name sadly became even more familiar the following season when he and the England winger, Reg Forest, along with a member of the English Rugby Union committee, R.S. Walley, contracted typhoid during their team's visit to Dublin for a Championship match. Oughtred was the only one of the three to survive.) Strand-Jones converted the resultant penalty with a drop goal to give the visitors victory at Blackheath for the first time in six attempts, which saw them embark once again on a successful Triple Crown and Championship campaign.

At the dinner following Wales's final victory that season against Ireland, by 15–0, one of the local administrators begrudgingly complained that the Wales team had the advantage of being in better condition than their opponents because their players in the main were ordinary workmen whose employment demanded a certain physicality (as opposed to players from the other countries in the Championship who had mostly been educated at public schools). Indeed the referee for the game in question against Ireland, Crawford Findlay, in a conversation with Rhys Gabe, said that he was surprised that Wales selected the likes of miners, steelworkers and policemen for the national rugby union team as they would be more suited to play rugby league in the Northern Union!

This attitude was further highlighted when it was revealed that the Irish Rugby Union had allocated £50 for the official dinner following their game with Scotland in 1902, but only £30 for the corresponding function after the Wales game. They explained that the reason for this was that the Scots had been given champagne, whereas the Wales players were supplied with beer. The Scots, it was said, 'were gentlemen and appreciated a dinner when it was given to them'. Not so the Welsh apparently!

One of the Scottish 'gentlemen' who played against Ireland that day was David Bedell-Sivright. He was the skipper of the British Isles team to Australia in 1904 and became the country's amateur heavyweight boxing champion. Following the official dinner after a previous game for Scotland, he chose to lie down for an hour across busy tram lines in Edinburgh, during which time the local policemen were too afraid to ask him to move. He did eventually get up, however, only to race over to a nearby cab-rank and tackle a horse!

8

10 January 1903: St Helen's, Swansea

21–5: Wales won by 5 tries and 3 conversions to 1 try and 1 conversion

Wales: J. Strand-Jones (Llanelli); W.F. Jowett, D. Rees (Swansea), R.T. Gabe (Llanelli), +T.W. Pearson; G.L. Lloyd (Newport), R.M. Owen (Swansea); J.G. Boots, J.J. Hodges (Newport), A.B. Brice (Aberavon), W. Joseph (Swansea), A.F. Harding (London Welsh), D. Jones (Treherbert), T. Osborne (Mountain Ash), G. Travers (Pill Harriers).

England: H.T. Gamlin (Devonport Albion); J.H. Miles (Leicester), J.T. Taylor (Castleford), R.H. Spooner (Liverpool), T. Simpson (Rockcliff); F.C. Hulme (Birkenhead Park), +B. Oughtred (Hartlepool Rovers); R. Bradley, J. Duthie (West Hartlepool), D.D. Dobson (Newton Abbot), G. Fraser (Richmond). R.F.A. Hobbs (Blackheath), P.F. Hardwick (Percy Park), R.D. Wood (Liverpool OB), V.H. Cartwright (Nottingham).

On an atrociously wet day, when the band had to leave the field before the kick-off because their instruments were being filled with rain-water, Wales recorded their fifth successive win against England before a crowd of 30,000. They were in no small way indebted to Jehoida Hodges, the burly Newport forward, for their victory, for he crossed for three tries in the first half, a record which has never been matched by any other forward in the history of the Championship. Indeed no other Welsh player succeeded in scoring three tries in one game until Maurice Richards in 1969. Yet it was a chance occurrence that placed Hodges in a position to set such a record.

Reference was made in the previous match report to the ferocious tackling of the England full-back, H.T. Gamlin, and to the manner in which he flattened Rhys Gabe as the winger crossed for the opening Wales try. He was later described by Gabe as 'a gorilla of a man with a devastating tackle'. The Wales left wing and captain for the 1903 fixture was Tommy Pearson. The previous season he had announced his retirement from rugby but after a short absence from the game he had been pressed by his club to resume playing. Consequently, due to an injury to the Wales captain, Gwyn Nicholls, the selectors asked Pearson to skipper his country for the game in question, thus earning his 13th cap and his first for five years (which also turned out to be his last), at the age of 31 years. Wales were further depleted in the three-quarter line by the absence also of Willie Llewellyn and Teddy Morgan.

Yet they made an auspicious start when Gabe passed to Pearson for the winger to cross for the first Welsh try. However, after 25 minutes of the match, Pearson tangled with full-back Gamlin and was forced to leave the field with two broken ribs, whereupon Jehoida Hodges was taken out of the pack to play on the wing in his place. Some critics were of the opinion that Gabe, perhaps subconsciously remembering the injury which he had suffered as a result of a Gamlin tackle in the previous game against England, had passed the ball to Pearson a little too early, thus allowing Gamlin to get to the Wales captain.

Yet Hodges could have no complaints regarding the manner in which Gabe put him away for each of his three tries. The Wales centre, on every one of those occasions, delayed his final pass, so that the England full-back was totally committed to tackling him, thus putting Hodges on a clear path to the line. As a result Gabe, too, suffered from the 'Gamlin effect' and later admitted that he came off the field at the end 'as sore and bruised as if I had been mauled by a bear'!

Remarkably, thanks also to a try by Dickie Owen and three conversions by Strand-Jones, Wales led by 21–0 at the interval. England's only reply was a try late in the game by the former Oxford Blue, Denys Dobson, converted by Taylor. The following year Dobson made history for a much more notorious reason. When playing for the British Isles in a provincial match against the Northern Districts in Newcastle, Australia, he became the first touring British player to be sent off.

However the incident was engulfed in controversy. Dobson was ordered from the field for swearing at the referee, Harry Dolan. The touring side's captain, David Bedell-Sivright, retired his team to their changing room in protest, insisting that they would only return if Dobson was allowed to continue playing. He was however forced to capitulate and, after a delay of 20 minutes, he took his team back onto the field, without Dobson. Having already lost one player through injury they continued with just 13 men, yet still won the game by 17–3.

According to his captain Dobson was one of the 'quietest and most gentlemanly members of the team' and at an enquiry convened later by the New South Wales Rugby Union, the errant forward claimed that all he had said to the referee, upon the award of yet another free kick to the home team, was 'What the devil was that for?' He was in due course cleared of the alleged offence of 'using indecent language towards the referee' and his infringement downgraded to 'using an improper expression'. Dobson never represented England again and when his career as a player came to an end he obtained a posting as a colonial officer in Nyasaland (nowadays Malawi). There, in 1916, he was sadly killed by a charging rhinoceros at the age of 35 years. It is claimed that when one of his former lecturers at Oxford heard the news he remarked that 'Dobson always had a weak hand-off'!

9

14 January 1905: Arms Park, Cardiff

25–0: Wales won by 7 tries and 2 conversions to nil

Wales: G. Davies (Swansea); +W.M. Llewellyn (Newport), D. Rees (Swansea), R.T. Gabe (Cardiff), E. Morgan (London Welsh); R. Jones, R.M. Owen; W. Joseph (Swansea), G. Travers (Pill Harriers), W. O'Neill (Cardiff), A.F. Harding (London Welsh), D. Jones (Treherbert), J.J. Hodges, C.M. Pritchard (Newport), H. Watkins (Llanelli).

England: S.H. Irvin (Devonport Albion); F.H. Palmer (Richmond), J.E. Raphael (OMT), E.W. Dillon, S.F. Cooper (Blackheath); W.V. Butcher (Bristol), F.C. Hulme (Birkenhead Park); +F.M. Stout (Richmond), J.L. Mathias (Bristol), V.H. Cartwright (Nottingham), B.A. Hill, W.T.C. Cave, C.J. Newbold, W.L.Y. Rogers (Blackheath), T.A. Gibson (Northern).

This was the sixth time in the last seven games between the two countries that England had been on the losing side, the other match ending in a draw. However, none of the other encounters had resulted in such a comprehensive defeat for the visitors. Indeed this was their worst result in a Championship match until they lost by 12–37 to France in 1972. The score also entailed that this was the greatest number of tries conceded by England in one match, until Wales scored eight against them in 1922. In 1905 Wales again went on to win the Triple Crown and the Championship.

The Swansea half-backs, Dick Jones and Dickie Owen (known as 'the dancing Dicks' by their club supporters), played havoc with the English defence. The service provided by scrum- half Owen gave his fly-half partner scope to confuse the opposition with a variety of attacking ploys. Such were the problems that they caused Sam Irvin, the visitors' full-back, who was winning his first cap, that he was never selected for his country again and eventually signed to play rugby league with Oldham. In contrast, George Davies, who had previously won six caps in the centre, had a splendid match at full-back for Wales, yet converted just two of the seven tries scored, by Morgan (2), Gabe, Harding, Dick Jones, Llewellyn and Watkins.

The dazzling play of the Wales backs produced five tries, yet it was the one scored by forward Harry Watkins that was the most memorable, when he ran from the halfway to touch down. Indeed the contribution of the pack to the victory was immense in that they dominated their English counterparts to provide ample possession for their backs. The amount of ball won from the scrum had improved significantly due to the fact that the selectors, displaying a considerable degree of rugby vision, had decided the previous season that they would select one of the forwards as a specialist hooker

Prior to that, teams had established the practice whereby, with regard to scrum-formation, the forwards packed down in the order in which they arrived at the scene, thus making rather a lottery of possession from the scrum. The hooker in question was George Travers, a coal-trimmer at Newport Docks, who played at the time for Pill Harriers, a second-class club. Over the next eight years he became one of the most established Welsh forwards, winning 25 caps in all.

It had been 20 years since another Welsh innovation, namely the deployment of a four-man three-quarter line instead of three. Its merits were amply illustrated in the game in question and had made a significant impact on the way the game was played. Yet although the other IRB countries had followed Wales in due course, some English critics, after the heavy defeat of 1905, lamented the fact that their backs hadn't yet grasped the advantages that the new system offered, and consequently advocated they return to the forward-orientated pattern of play which would be facilitated by resorting to a nine-man pack.

One of the Welsh players who revelled in the freedom given to the three-quarters was winger Dr Teddy Morgan. His talents had been recognised by the British Isles selectors the previous year when he was chosen to play in four Tests against Australia and then New Zealand, having been made captain in all but the first Test. Despite his diminutive build – he stood just 5' 7" and weighed 12 stone – he was remarkably fast. He crossed for two tries in the 1905 match and in all touched down on 14 occasions for his country in 16 games. However, his greatest claim to fame was scoring the winning try later that year, with a combination of guile and remarkable pace, when Wales defeated the All Blacks by 3–0, the only loss suffered by the New Zealanders in 35 matches played during their tour that year. His reputation was further enhanced when he later prevented what would have been an equalising try by Bob Deans, an incident which became shrouded in controversy.

He had, however, made a notable contribution before the game had started, when, following the *haka* performed by the All Blacks, Morgan led his team in a chorus of 'Hen Wlad Fy Nhadau', which was picked up by the crowd, thus starting the practice of singing the national anthem at the start of international sporting fixtures.

10

13 January 1906: Richmond

16–3: Wales won by 4 tries and 2 conversions to
1 try

Wales: H.B. Winfield (Cardiff); H.T. Maddock (London Welsh),
+E.G. Nicholls, R.T. Gabe (Cardiff), E. Morgan (London Welsh);
P.F. Bush (Cardiff), R.M. Owen (Swansea); Cliff Pritchard
(Pontypool) rover back; W. Joseph (Swansea), G. Travers
(Pill Harriers), H. Watkins (Llanelli), A.F. Harding (London
Welsh), D. Jones (Aberdare), J.J. Hodges, Charlie M. Pritchard
(Newport).

England. E.J. Jacket (Falmouth), A.E. Hind (Leicester),
J.E. Raphael (OMT), H.E. Shewring (Bristol), A. Hudson
(Gloucester); R.A. Jago (Devonport Albion), D.R. Gent
(Gloucester); +V.A. Cartwright, H.A. Hodges (Nottingham),
C.E.L. Hammond (Harlequins), A.L. Kewney (Rockcliff), T.S.
Kelly (Exeter), W.A. Mills, G.E. Dobbs (Devonport Albion),
E.W. Roberts (RNC Dartmouth).

The All Blacks had left Britain in 1905 following their first
ever tour of the home countries, having made an indelible
impression with their skilful, powerful and innovative style
of play. As a result the 1906 Championship saw an attempt
by two of the teams, Wales and Ireland, to adopt new
methods with a view to improving playing standards. This
match, therefore, saw the visitors play just seven men in
their pack, and eight backs, one of whom was classified as
a 'rover'. This was a tactic that Wales had learned from the
All Blacks and had initially applied in their victory against
them in 1905. In addition, having already designated George
Travers as a specialist hooker in 1904, they now proceeded
to allot other players to specialised positions in the scrum.

45

In that connection, in this particular game, Travers had two designated props packing down on either side of him. England's only attempt at innovation for the match was to select ten new caps, one of whom, full-back E.J. Jacket, was a nude artist's model and a cycling champion of Great Britain.

Indeed the new Welsh scrum formation formed a much more cohesive unit than their English counterparts and provided a sufficiently solid platform, despite their numerical disadvantage, to enable the Welsh backs to work their customary magic. Their orchestrator was outside-half Percy Bush, who, following a very impressive debut against the All Blacks the previous month, was playing in his first Championship match.

His rise to fame had been remarkably sudden. Having excelled for East Wales vs West Wales in 1904, he was chosen shortly afterwards to tour Australia and New Zealand with the British Isles team, where he became one of the party's star players and a darling of the crowds, particularly in Australia. *125 Years of the British and Irish Lions* quotes a rugby correspondent in that country at the time:

> The champion of the visitors is Percy Bush... When Bush gets the leather from the half-back he does not immediately pass the ball, but he begins propping and dodging from side to side... When he gets clear he can run like a deer, and sometimes he runs clean away from comrades and opponents alike, and generally ends up scoring himself... Without Bush I don't think the Britishers would be nearly the strong team they are, for he opens up all the work for the backs and always beats a couple of men before he gets rid of the ball.

In the same vein the *New Zealand Times* described 'the little Welshman, Percy Bush' as standing out over the other players. He played in all but one of the 19 matches on the tour, scoring in 14 of them, with a final total of 110 points which included 11 tries. Injury prevented his appearing for Wales in the 1904–5 Championship but following the 1906 victory against

England he perhaps surprisingly represented his country in only seven other international matches, winning his last cap in 1910. He was also an excellent cricketer and played for Glamorgan County Cricket Club and the MCC. He was reputed to be a mischievous 'cheeky chappie' whose chatter was often incessant. A school teacher by profession, in 1910 he also became British Vice-Consul in Nantes and that year, when playing rugby for the town, scored 54 points himself (including 10 tries) against Le Havre!

Despite the significant contribution of Bush to the penetrative running of the Welsh backs in the 1906 victory the playing of Cliff Pritchard as a 'rover' was not considered to have been a great success as he tended to clutter the midfield and consequently impede, at times, the effectiveness of the three-quarters. Nevertheless, the backs did score two tries, one the result of a typical Teddy Morgan dash for the line, the other by his club colleague and Welsh debutant playing on the opposite wing, Hopcyn Maddocks, which was the first of his six tries in six appearances for his country. The first try was the result of a charge-down by Jehoida Hodges, with Charlie Pritchard getting the other Welsh try. The Gloucester winger Arthur Hudson touched down for England's only score. Yet there were some who considered the final tally to be perhaps a little unfair on the home team.

Regardless of their comprehensive victory, the Welsh tactic in this particular match of playing seven backs plus a rover, with just seven forwards, had not convinced its detractors. Indeed the next encounter against Scotland in Cardiff, even though it was won by Wales by 9–3, further fuelled their doubts. For in that game the seven-man home pack was no match for the powerful Scottish eight which served to underline the fact that the new system was still at an experimental stage.

11

12 January 1907: St Helen's, Swansea

22–0: Wales won by 6 tries and 2 conversions to nil

Wales: D. Bailey Davies (Llanelli); J.L. Williams, R.T. Gabe (Cardiff), J.H. Evans (Pontypool), H.T. Maddocks (London Welsh); R.A. Gibbs (Cardiff), W.J. Trew, +R.M. Owen (Swansea); W. Neill (Cardiff), G. Travers (Pill Harriers), J. Brown (Cardiff), T. Evans, J. Watts (Llanelli), Charlie M. Pritchard, W. Dowell (Newport).

England: E.J. Jacket (Falmouth); S.F. Coopper (Blackheath), J.G.G. Birkett (Harlequins), H.E. Shewring, F.S. Scott (Bristol); A.D. Stoop (Harlequins), R. Jago (Devonport Albion); +B.A. Hill, F.J. Hopley (Blackheath), C.H. Shaw (Moseley), L.A.N. Slocock (Liverpool), W.A. Mills (Devonport Albion), T.S. Kelly (Exeter), W.M. Nanson (Carlisle), J. Green (Skipton).

Following their defeat against Scotland the previous season, Wales had shelved their eight backs plus seven forwards formation for their last game in the Championship against Ireland in Belfast. For that game they reverted to the eight forwards pattern but were nonetheless defeated after a poor performance. Therefore, for the opening game against England in 1907, they adopted another recent innovation, and selected two outside-halves, as they had done during the previous season against Scotland. The decision was indeed justified in that the Wales backs, in front of a disappointingly small crowd of 12,000, sparkled in scoring five of their team's six tries. The try scorers were Maddocks (2), Williams (2), Brown and Gibbs, with the latter also kicking two conversions

Much was expected from the visitors, since, in a fixture against France (who did not officially become part of the Championship until 1910) the previous week they had scored nine tries in a 41–13 victory. Yet in this game at St Helen's they were well beaten and their pack rendered impotent by a dominant Wales seven who provided an ample supply of ball to set their half-backs alight. Remarkably, the home team had been in a similar position to their opponents in their previous match against the touring South Africans six weeks earlier. On that occasion, in front of 40,000 supporters, Wales had been on the receiving end of a comprehensive beating when they were completely outplayed and their pack demolished. The occasion was described at the time as one of the darkest days in the history of Welsh rugby.

Perhaps the main architect of England's downfall in 1907 was Dicky Owen, the Swansea scrum-half, who was making his first appearance as captain of the national side. He did not skipper the side again until five years later when, against England, he represented his country for the 34th time, which was a record. He played once more in the red jersey and his 35 caps went unsurpassed until 1955 when the Newport winger, Ken Jones, broke his record.

Owen, alongside Haydn Tanner and Gareth Edwards perhaps, was rated as one of the best ever Welsh scrum-halves. His build in no way suggested that he was such a talented performer. He was just 5' 4" tall and weighed 9 stones 7 lbs, which made him one of the smallest players to have ever played for Wales, yet, as his sobriquets 'the pocket Hercules' and 'the mighty midget' suggest, he relished the physical challenges with which he was regularly confronted. He was an innovative player in that he constantly sought to devise new strategies for scrum-half play and in that connection he became a pioneer of, for example, moves which saw him link with his wing forwards or feinting to run or pass.

His distribution was swift and accurate (another of his sobriquets was 'the Bullet') and he considered his main role to be a provider and orchestrator for players outside him. He was also credited with being the perfector of the reverse pass, a skill which he applied to great effect in instigating Wales's only score in their victory over the 1905 All Blacks. This particular talent was indicative of his readiness at all times to try the unconventional and the unexpected. This characteristic, on another level, was also evident in the match against England in 1904. Daunted by the fact that the Scottish referee, Crawford Findlay (see page 38), had awarded England countless penalties for scrum offences by Wales during the first half, Owen, for the remainder of the game, opted to allow his English counterpart to feed every scrum, even when it was a Welsh put-in!

He was also made captain in his final game for Wales against Scotland in 1912 and was carried shoulder-high from the field. A former milkman and then steel worker by profession, he became, on his retirement from rugby, a publican in Swansea, where in 1932, at the age of 55, he sadly committed suicide.

12

18 January 1908: Ashton Gate, Bristol

28–18: Wales won by 5 tries, 3 conversions, 1 penalty goal and 1 drop goal to 4 tries and 3 conversions

Wales: H.B. Winfield; J.L. Williams, R.T. Gabe (Cardiff), W.J. Trew (Swansea), R.A. Gibbs; P.F. Bush (Cardiff), T.H. Vile (Newport); J. Webb (Abertillery), G. Travers (Pill Harriers), W. Neill, J. Brown (Cardiff), J. Watts (Llanelli), Charlie M. Pritchard (Newport), W. Dowell (Pontypool), +A.F. Harding (London Welsh).

England: A.E. Wood (Gloucester); D. Lambert, +J.G.G. Birkett (Harlequins), W.N. Lapage (United Services), A. Hudson (Gloucester); J. Peters (Plymouth), R.H. Williamson (Oxford Univ.); R. Gilbert, W. Mills (Devonport Albion), F. Boylen, H. Havelock (Hartlepool Rovers), L.A.N. Slocock (Liverpool), C.E.L. Hammond, G.D. Roberts (Harlequins), R. Dibble (Bridgwater Albion).

For this game England fielded seven new caps, while Wales opted for a settled team with just one debutant. The home side included, for the first time in the Championship, a coloured player, Jim Peters, who was selected at outside-half.

The match was played in front of a crowd of 25,000, yet a large number of them frustratingly had no idea as to what was happening on the field. A thick fog had descended on the ground giving sometimes an eerie appearance to the players as they fleetingly came and went like phantoms before the spectators. Similarly, from the centre of the field, the spectators were invisible to the players. Those on the field had to listen carefully to discover where the ball was bouncing, since it was impossible to follow it with their eyes, or had to judge the location of a particular play from the shouting of their fellow players. When asked by the press before the game which way Wales would be playing in the first half Percy Bush, the Wales outside-half, replied 'With the fog!'

There were other amusing tales resulting from the misty conditions. At half-time, when Bush went missing, he was found in the crowd chatting to the spectators. At the end of the game the players were having their bath when it was realised that full-back Bert Winfield was not with them. One of the Welsh officials went to look for him and, upon calling his name, found that he was still out on the pitch, lost in the fog and thinking that the game was still in progress with the play at the other end of the field!

Perhaps aided by the conditions, the game apparently turned out to be very entertaining with plenty of deceptive running! The Wales outside-half, Percy Bush, with his dodging, penetrative sorties, was a difficult player for opponents to deal with at the best of times, but in the fog of Ashton Gate he was an even bigger nightmare! At one point in the game he and Rhys Gabe went to gather a loose ball on their opponents' 25-yard line, whereupon Bush shot off for the England goal-line to disappear in the mist with the England defence in his wake. In due course the referee and some of the players arrived at the goal-line to find Gabe waiting there with the ball, having touched down for a try.

Bush was ably assisted on the day by the debutant scrum-half Tommy Vile of Newport, an excellent player who unfortunately was a contemporary of the brilliant Dicky Owen. Vile was another who had appeared in Tests for the British Isles team (on their tour of Australia and New Zealand in 1904) before being selected for Wales. Despite his slender build, his pedigree as a sturdy, rugged performer was earned during his early days at Newport where he played in the pack. Some three years later he settled for the scrum-half position and soon acquired a reputation as an excellent passer of the ball and a very able kicker, with a particular talent for kicking drop goals.

Despite playing very well at Ashton Gate, Vile, after just one more game, lost his place to Dicky Owen, who was returning from injury, for the remainder of the international season. However, when Owen retired from international rugby in 1912, Vile was recalled for four games before being dropped again, only to return to the national team as captain against Scotland in 1921. He was one of seven players who represented Wales before and after the First World War. He became a referee shortly afterwards, eventually taking charge of 12 international matches. In 1945 he became High Sheriff of Monmouthshire and, ten years later, president of the WRU.

With both sides being credited with playing well in the 1908 fixture, Wales crossed for five tries to England's four. The scorers for the visitors were all backs with Gabe (2), Bush Gibbs and Trew getting the touch downs. Winfield (2) and Bush kicked conversions, with Bush also converting a drop goal and Winfield a penalty. Although Wales were always ahead, the home team were never far behind with Birkett (2), Lapage and Williamson getting their tries. Wood (2) and Roberts kicked conversions with the latter (following the Second World War he became a prosecutor at the Nuremberg trials) underlining the difficulties facing all the kickers that day when he complained that the posts would disappear in the mist as he ran up to kick the ball!

With this game Wales overtook England for the first time with regard to the number of victories they had achieved against each other, having now recorded 12 wins to England's 11, with two drawn matches.

13

16 January 1909: Arms Park, Cardiff
8–0: Wales won by 2 tries and 1 conversion to nil

Wales: J. Bancroft (Swansea); J.L. Williams (Cardiff), P. Jones (Newport), +W.J. Trew, P. Hopkins; R. Jones, R.M. Owen (Swansea); T. Evans (Llanelli), G. Travers (Pill Harriers), P.D. Waller (Newport), J. Brown (Cardiff), J. Webb, J. Blackmore (Abertillery), G. Hayward, I. Morgan (Swansea).

England: E.J. Jackett (Leicester); B.B. Bennetts (Penzance), F.N. Tarr (Leicester), E.R. Mobbs (Northampton), E.W. Assinder (Old Edwardians); J. Davey (Redruth), T.G. Wedge (St Ives); +R. Dibble (Bridgwater), A.L. Kewney (Rockcliff), J.G. Cooper (Moseley), A.D.W. Morris (United Services), W. Johns (Gloucester), E.D. Ibbitson (Headingley), F.G. Handford (Manchester), H. Archer (Guy's Hospital).

This was the beginning of another successful Triple Crown and Grand Slam campaign for Wales, which they had achieved for the first time in 1908. They fielded six new caps, to the visitors' 11, and although they won this particular match through tries by wingers Hopkins and Williams, they were soundly beaten at forward.

One of the tries was converted by Jack Bancroft, a younger brother of the famous W.J. Bancroft, and who was representing his country for the first time. He played in place of Bert Winfield, who had to withdraw from the team as a result of an injury to his thumb. Jack Bancroft went on to win 18 caps and became one of the legendary figures of Welsh rugby. His more flamboyant brother had scored 60 international points for Wales in 33 games. However this was bettered by Jack in only his 14th match for his country before going on to accumulate a tally of 88 points by the end of his international career.

Jack played in his last match in 1914, at the age of 35, when the outbreak of war put an end to the Home Nations Championship until 1920, and when his particular game was not so reliable as it used to be. This brought an end to an era during which, in the 102 internationals that Wales had played up until then, a Bancroft had appeared at full-back in 51 of those games. During the latter part of Jack's career France had joined the Home Championship and a significant number of the points he scored in the red jersey were attained in the four matches he played against them. Indeed in the 1910 fixture he scored 19 points, a record which stood until equalled by firstly Keith Jarrett in 1967 and then by Phil Bennett in 1976. It was only bettered in 1990 when Paul Thorburn scored 21 points against the Barbarians, a match for which the players were controversially awarded full caps by the WRU.

Jack Bancroft was a steady, reliable full-back who rarely displayed any flair. Despite his points-scoring ability he was probably more renowned for his courage in defence. Following the Wales defeat at Twickenham three years later, his contribution to the game was described thus by A.A. Thomson, the celebrated sports journalist, who attended the match as a boy:

> ... he seemed frequently to be playing the whole English team by himself... Frequently, looking like a lone defender, he performed the task of half-a-dozen men, tackling and kicking as if he had as many arms and legs as a Hindu deity.

The author Huw Richards notes that when Thomson, having told a friend that he had seen 'the Great Bancroft' play, was informed that Jack was merely the great W.B. Bancroft's little brother. In response, the future journalist retorted that Bill, therefore, must have had wings in addition! Like his brother, Jack was also an accomplished cricketer and played for Glamorgan on several occasions as a wicket-keeper batsman.

Also making his first appearance in the 1909 victory

against England was hooker, Phil Waller, who travelled with the British Isles team to South Africa in 1910 and played in all three Tests. He stayed on after the tour, later joining the South Africa Heavy Artillery Regiment which resulted in his death in 1917 when fighting in the First World War.

14

21 January 1911: St Helen's, Swansea

15–11: Wales won by 4 tries and 1 penalty goal to 3 tries and 1 conversion

Wales: J. Bancroft (Swansea); J.L. Williams, W. Spiller (Cardiff), F.W. Birt (Newport), R.A. Gibbs (Cardiff); +W.J. Trew, R.M. Owen (Swansea); J. Webb (Abertillery), J. Pugsley (Cardiff), A.P. Coldrick (Newport), H. Jarman (Pontypool), W. Perry (Neath), T. Evans (Llanelli), D.J. Thomas, I. Morgan (Swansea).

England: S.H. Williams (Newport); A.D. Roberts (Northern), J.A. Scholfield (Preston Grasshoppers), +J.G.G. Birkett, D. Lambert; A.D. Stoop (Harlequins), A.L.H. Gotley (Blackheath); A.L. Kewney (Leicester), J.A. King (Headingley), R. Dibble (Bridgwater), W.E. Mann, N.A. Wodehouse (United Services), L. Haigh (Manchester), L.G. Brown, C.H. Pillman (Blackheath).

Perhaps anticipating a much closer encounter than usual, following England's first victory against Wales for the previous 11 years in the mud at Twickenham in 1910, 40,000 spectators turned up for this particular game with the demand for tickets exceeding the number available. Indeed the match set the scene for a particularly exciting Championship which led to Wales winning the Triple Crown (a feat however which they would not accomplish again until 1950) and the Grand Slam, which was the first time the latter had been achieved in a Five Nations Championship competition. In the opinion of many critics it was the greatest ever, with 55 tries (of which Wales had scored 18) in a total of 247 points. The number of tries has yet to be exceeded in the Championship and the points total remained a record until the value of the try was raised to four points in 1972, when 249 points were scored.

The match was closely fought with Wales being pressurised

throughout by their opponents which led Billy Trew, the home skipper, to declare later that it was the finest England team that he had ever played against. At times there was a distinctive lack of *hwyl* in the Wales performance and at half-time they led by just 9–6, following tries by Gibbs and Spiller and a penalty goal by Birt. However, immediately after the restart, a brilliant piece of interplay by Dickie Owen (who in the opinion of many critics had probably his finest game for Wales that day) and Trew saw Wales go further ahead. Working the blind side from a scrum near the England line, Owen fed his outside-half who, in drawing Williams, the England full-back from Newport, was knocked out in the tackle, but not before releasing the speedy Swansea flanker Ivor Morgan to cross for a try. England hit back with a converted try and while Wales were leading by 12–11 late into the second half, the game at that stage could have gone either way, with the visitors gradually gaining the upper hand. However, a try by Joe Pugsley, the Newport forward, during the closing stages, ensured a Welsh victory.

The game saw Harold Jarman make his final appearance for his country after winning just four caps. Yet during the British Isles visit to South Africa in 1910 he proved to be one of the stars of the tourists' pack. He was one of seven Newport players to make the trip, five of whom had been capped by Wales, with the England full-back, Williams, and the Irish forward, Dr Tom Smyth (who captained the tourists) completing the Gwent contingent. Jarman played in all three Tests and was greatly admired, particularly by the South Africans, for his display in the victory by the British Isles in the second Test. His ruggedness and mobility around the field were attributes which were greatly valued by Springbok rugby followers.

In 1928 some children were playing on a colliery tramway at Talywain near Pontypool when a runaway tram careered towards them. Jarman, who worked as a blacksmith at the pit-head, on seeing the impending danger threw himself in front of the tram in order that his body would cause it to be derailed, thus saving the children from serious and possibly fatal injuries. Although he survived the immediate collision, his injuries ultimately caused complications which sadly led to his death just before Christmas that year, at the age of 45 years.

In the 1911 game perhaps the lack of *hwyl* in the Wales performance was a reflection of the disinterest that had prevailed amongst the crowd even before the game. There were references in the press to the fact there was a distinct absence, before the kick-off, of singing and any kind of fervour at St Helen's. Indeed the highlight of the pre-match entertainment, according to the *Western Mail*, was:

> ... the appearance of an acrobatic performer, who is well known on Welsh football grounds, entering the arena with a bicycle and a couple of chairs. He was about to begin his performance when Mr. Walter Rees [secretary of the WRU] crossed the ground. The acrobat disregarded the order from Mr. Rees to leave, then proceeded to go through his evolutions. Mr. Rees promptly called the police, but even then the acrobat refused to leave. After one policeman had taken away the chairs, and another had wheeled off the bicycle, it required the combined forces of seven constables to carry the entertainer off the ground, amidst the vigorous booing of the crowd. The spectators became quite angry and the police who were stationed at different points along the touchline, were pelted with oranges and subjected to all manner of derision.

So, just as the Wales supporters at the game against the All Blacks in 1905 are accredited with the inception of the singing of national anthems at international matches, it could be said that spectators at this 1911 match at Swansea were perhaps the instigators of crowd disorder at such events!

15

17 January 1920: St Helen's, Swansea

19–5: Wales won by 2 tries, 1 conversion, 2 drop goals and 1 penalty goal to 1 try and 1 conversion

Wales: J. Rees (Swansea); W.J. Powell (Cardiff), J. Shea (Newport), A. Jenkins, B. Evans (Llanelli); B. Beynon (Swansea), J. Wetter (Newport); J. Williams (Blaina), +H. Uzzell, J. Whitfield (Newport), S. Morris (Cross Keys), G. Oliver (Pontypool), T. Parker (Swansea), J. Jones (Aberavon), C.W. Jones (Bridgend).

England: B.S. Cumberlege (Blackheath); H.L.V. Day (Leicester), E.D.G. Hammett (Newport), J.A. Krige (Guy's Hospital), C.N. Lowe; H. Coverdale (Blackheath), C.A. Kershaw (United Services); G. Holford, S. Smart (Gloucester), J.R. Morgan (Hawick), W.H.G. Wright (Plymouth), L.P.B. Merriam, F.W. Mellish (Blackheath), W.W. Wakefield (Harlequins), +J.E. Greenwood (Cambridge Univ.).

Upon the resumption of Championship fixtures between the two countries following the First World War, this was the first Wales victory over England since 1911. The match naturally saw a large number of players from both teams make their debuts for their countries. There were 11 new caps in the visitors' team whereas all but two of the Wales team were wearing the red jersey for the first time. One of those players, Jerry Shea, the Newport centre, created a record in scoring 16 points by every possible means, which in this instance amounted to one try, one conversion, two drop goals and a penalty goal. This was a feat which remained unequalled by a Welsh player in the Championship until Neil Jenkins scored 28 points in every possible manner against France in 2001.

There were many interesting selections on both sides. Ernest Dyer Galbraith Hammett, of Newport, had been born in Somerset yet was invited to play in the centre for Wales alongside his club colleague, Shea. However, despite his preference for the home side, he declined the WRU's invitation since he had previously agreed to play for England on the day. Doubtless the home selectors had been encouraged to secure Hammett's allegiance by the fact that he had previously represented Wales at tennis and at soccer, having won an amateur cap against England while playing for Treharris. Hammett went on to play on seven other occasions for England.

In the Welsh line-up there were several noteworthy inclusions. Playing at outside-half, and on his home ground, was Ben Beynon, who became the 300th player to represent his country at rugby union. He was also an accomplished soccer player with Swansea Town and scored the only goal of the game to knock Blackburn Rovers out of the FA Cup in 1915, despite being the only amateur on the pitch. He played for Wales in the next Championship game against Scotland in 1920 but by then he had accepted an offer to play professionally for the Swans in the Southern League, for £6 a week, as well as being allowed to keep his job at a local tinplate works. Consequently, in the eyes of the WRU, he was now a professional and had to forfeit his rugby international cap as well as his Swansea Rugby Club cap and blazer.

The following season Swansea Town were promoted to the Football League and Beynon became their second highest scorer. Having attested that rugby was always his first love, he moved to Oldham Rugby League Club in 1922, for a fee of £325. In four seasons he scored 77 points in 94 games and won a Challenge Cup winner's medal with the club in 1925, before returning to Wales the following year to resume playing soccer.

Another player winning his first cap in 1920, in the centre, was the Llanelli legend Albert Jenkins, who, after an illustrious career for club and country, was given a civic burial by his home town when he passed away in 1953 at the age of 58. He made his first appearance for the Scarlets just four months before this game. He went on to win 14 caps in all, over a period of nine years, which was surprising in the light of his remarkable talent. Stradey supporters would claim that the Welsh selectors were always biased in favour of players from east Wales, yet it was also said that his form away from his beloved home patch could be erratic.

Nevertheless he had undoubted qualities which also attracted many unsuccessful bids from rugby league clubs for his services. Firstly, he possessed remarkable strength, an attribute which was nurtured in his occupation, firstly as a loader at the Llanelli North Dock, where it was said that he handled bags of potatoes as if they were packets of crisps, then as a coal trimmer and tinplate worker. He had exceptionally large hands which made easy work of taking the ball one-handed at pace. He was also a powerful runner with a particular penchant for bursting at speed, often from a standing start, through prospective tackles, with his sturdy thighs making him very difficult to bring down. Even when he could be knocked over his stocky, barrel-chested build, measuring 5' 8" and weighing 12½ stone, and an ability to regain his feet with surprising agility, often allowed him to continue on his destructive path.

Yet he was also blessed with more refined skills, enabling him to punish the opposition as required with graceful and balanced running. In addition, he was a very effective kicker from the hand, an accurate place-kicker, and an excellent passer of the ball. He also had the ability to read a game in such a manner as to play decisively on the apparent weaknesses of opponents. It was perhaps no wonder that he was granted hero status in his home town and it was said that long queues would form outside Stradey on match days in the hope that there would be an opportunity to carry his bag.

With regard to this particular match, two of the debutants

in the Wales team had impressive pugilistic qualifications. George Oliver, the Pontypool forward, was the Welsh heavyweight amateur boxing champion, while Jerry Shea, in addition to being a sprinter and swimmer of no mean repute, was also an accomplished welterweight boxer, who a short time later unsuccessfully fought the world champion Ted Kid Lewis. Indeed he succeeded in beating other British and European champions such as Johnny Basham, René DeVos, Frank Moody and Gipsy Daniels.

There was drama in the visitors' camp before the game had even started. W.M. Lowry, the Birkenhead Park winger, had been selected to play on the wing and lined up with his fellow players for the team photo on the pitch prior to taking the field for the match. However, minutes before the teams ran out he was replaced by Harold Day, of Leicester, who had already settled in his seat in the stand to watch the game. The reasons given by the England selection committee for the late change were that Lowry had played poorly for Birkenhead the previous week and that the playing surface at St Helen's on the day was not firm enough to suit his particular game! Ironically, he had already been awarded his first cap in the changing room, but he did play in England's next game against France, his only appearance for his country.

The match at Swansea, played in atrociously wet conditions, saw Wales, captained by the 37-year-old Uzzell, take the lead through a penalty by Shea (which he kicked as a drop goal) against the wind. England replied with a try by Day, when Hammett, using his footballing talent to great effect to undertake a skilful dribble, crossed the ball soccer-style to see his winger score and add the conversion. England led 5–3 at the interval but soon after Shea regained the lead for his team with a drop kick. Although the Wales forwards were in control, the home team failed to capitalise until half way through the second period when Shea broke through the England defence to cross under the posts, giving him an easy conversion. Winger Powell then scored another try for Wales, following excellent work by Shea, before the latter completed a remarkable day's scoring with another drop goal to give Wales a well deserved victory.

Shea was carried shoulder-high from the field by delighted Wales supporters, yet critics had certain reservations concerning his performance. He was accused of selfishly going on his own too often and ignoring players outside him who, on several occasions, included Albert Jenkins, much to the disgust of the hordes of Llanelli supporters in the crowd. Shea's rather ungainly running style was also said to impede the attacking fluency of the Wales backs and despite his auspicious contribution to the score on the day he won just three more caps for his country.

16

21 January 1922: Arms Park, Cardiff

28–6: Wales won by 8 tries and 2 conversions to 2 tries

Wales: J. Rees (Swansea); C. Richards (Pontypool), B. Evans (Llanelli), I. Evans, F. Palmer; W. Bowen (Swansea), W.J. Delahay (Bridgend); +T. Parker (Swansea), J. Whitfield, T. Jones (Newport), S. Morris (Cross Keys), T. Roberts (Risca), Revd J.G. Stephens (Llanelli), W. Cummins (Treorchy), D. Hiddlestone (Neath).

England: B.S. Cumberlege (Blackheath); H.L.V. Day (Leicester), E. Myers (Bradford), E.D.G. Hammett, C.N. Lowe (Blackheath); V.G. Davies (Harlequins), C.A. Kershaw (United Services); +L.G. Brown (Blackheath), J.S. Tucker (Bristol), E.R. Gardner (Devonport Services), R. Edwards (Newport), G.S. Conway (Rugby), A.F. Blakiston (Northampton), W.W. Wakefield (Harlequins), A.T. Voyce (Gloucester).

Having been soundly beaten at Twickenham the previous season, when England won an impressive Grand Slam while conceding just nine points in four matches, Wales convincingly returned to their winning ways in scoring the greatest number of tries ever conceded by England. The match brought to an end a winning sequence of seven matches for the visitors, their last defeat having occurred against Wales two years previously.

Following this encounter Wales proceeded to win the Championship once again, for the ninth time, having also been runners-up on nine occasions. They were victorious in 42 of the 56 matches played until the 1921–2 season. Apart from the record number of tries scored by Wales in this particular match, another landmark was attained in that it was the first occasion, following an agreement reached the previous year by the rugby unions in question, on which players from both sides wore numbered jerseys in a Championship match.

England had arrived at Cardiff hoping to play their newly-found style of flowing rugby only to be thwarted by two particular factors, the first of which was the very muddy condition of the pitch. Wavel Wakefield, one of the stalwarts of English rugby who went on to win 31 caps for his country, stated that it was difficult to even stand up on the day since the ground was so slippery. On the other hand he noted that the Welsh team were more adequately prepared for such treacherous conditions by having exceptionally long studs on their boots, perhaps illegally so.

Notwithstanding the mud, the other more influential factor in effecting the downfall of the England team was the destructive, marauding efficiency of the Wales forwards and in particular the flankers. For the first time ever the home team deployed two specialist wing-forwards, one of whom, Dai Hiddlestone from the Neath club, was winning his first cap at the age of 32 years. He was the game's star performer, just as his grandson, Terry Price, in later years excelled for his country. Dai was known as 'the pocket battleship' and despite being only 5' 8" tall he successfully hounded the English backs throughout the game. He thwarted all their efforts to play open rugby, and forced them to change their fly-half in the second half in a fruitless endeavour to improve their fortunes.

That he displayed remarkable mobility and endurance in such difficult conditions was the result of his fanatical obsession with fitness. It was said that he would regularly undertake training runs after work in his home village of Hendy accompanied by his dog, but would have to continue on his own in due course as the dog would have returned home exhausted long before Dai had finished his stint!

He was one of eight new caps in the Wales team, in which there were also five players from the Swansea club, all of whom were among the try scorers. That list constituted the names of Whitfield, Bowen, Hiddlestone, Delahay, Palmer, Richards,

Parker, and Islwyn Evans, with Rees converting two of the tries. Evans played in every international that season and scored in all four games, with three tries and a drop goal to his name. Yet he never appeared again for his country.

Hiddlestone, having been discarded, like Islwyn Evans, by the Wales selectors for the Championship games the following season, was recalled in 1924 to play for his country for a fifth and final time against the touring All Blacks and was the cause of considerable controversy before the start of the game. In response to the traditional All Black *haka*, Dai took it upon himself to lead the Wales team in a kind of *ad hoc* war dance of their own, which was generally considered to be extremely offensive towards the tourists. His final link with the All Blacks, however, was in his capacity as a referee, when he took charge of the match between a combined Neath/Aberavon team and the 1935 New Zealand tourists.

Following the 1922 match between Wales and England the victory count was delicately balanced between the two sides, with 16 wins apiece. However, over the next few years, the fortunes of the previously extremely successful Wales side went into considerable decline which led to several mediocre displays.

17

16 January 1932: St Helen's, Swansea

12–5: Wales won by 1 try, 1 conversion, 1 drop goal and 1 penalty goal to 1 try and 1 conversion

Wales: +J. Bassett (Penarth); J.C. Morley (Newport), E.C. Davey (Swansea), F. Williams, R.W. Boon (Cardiff); A. Ralph (Newport), W.C. Powell (London Welsh); T. Day (Swansea), F.A. Bowdler (Cross Keys), A. Skym (Cardiff), E.M. Jenkins (Aberavon), D. Thomas, W. Davies, W. Thomas (Swansea), A. Lemon (Neath).

England: R.J. Barr (Leicester); C.C. Tanner (Gloucester), R.A. Gerrard (Bath), J.A. Tallent, +C.D. Aarvold (Blackheath); R.S. Spong, W.H. Sobey (Old Millhillians); G.G. Gregory (Bristol), D.J. Norman (Leicester), N.L. Evans (RNEC Devonport), R.G.S. Hobbs (Richmond), C.S.H. Webb (Devonport Services), L.E. Saxby (Gloucester), E. Coley (Northampton), J.McD. Hodgson (Northern).

This was the first Welsh success over England for ten years... which still represents the longest interval between victories for the men in red against the foe from across the border. This also represented a resurgence of form in that they had now been undefeated for seven successive games in the Championship and, in getting the better of Scotland also in their next game, their run represented their best sequence in the Championship until the early Seventies. However, like England, they had been beaten the previous month by the touring South Africans, which probably accounted for the comparatively disappointing attendance figure of 30,000. In a Championship which saw France excluded by the other home unions for failing to curb illegal payments to their club players (a ban which prevailed until 1947), Wales, Scotland and Ireland finished the season having suffered one defeat each.

The absence of France from the competition saw a dramatic fall in the number of tries scored each season. During their final appearance in the Championship in 1931 before their exclusion, 41 tries were scored by the five teams concerned. Over the next nine seasons (excluding the war period) the average number of tries scored by the four Championship teams was 18. This was not, of course, due to France's own contribution to the try total, but rather to the lack of opportunity afforded the other home nation sides to accumulate tries against them. For Les Bleus, notwithstanding their penchant for open, attacking rugby, had a regrettable reputation for being rather fragile in defence.

In the game in question Wales were by far the better side and their superiority should have been reflected by a much greater margin of victory. Perhaps an indication of England's disappointing display is the fact that five of their players were dropped for their next game against Ireland, whereas Wales fielded an unchanged team to oppose Scotland one month later. Even so, there was no score during the first half, before Wales started to convert their obvious ascendancy into points. They comfortably built a lead of 12–0, with England getting perhaps an undeserved consolation try when the Northampton Number 8, Eric Coley, charged over the line, a score which was greeted with great indignation by the crowd since it appeared that the referee had failed to spot a knock-on which had preceded the touch-down.

One of the outstanding contributors to the Wales performance was flanker Arthur Lemon. He harassed and plagued the highly regarded and talented outside-half, R.S. Spong, to such an extent that the Englishman stood deeper and deeper to take the ball as the game progressed, thus becoming increasingly ineffective. This was British Lion Spong's seventh and last cap for his country. Not only was the sturdy Lemon an extremely mobile wing-forward but also an excellent forager and spoiler. Indeed his strength and ruggedness were such that for the Ireland game the following season the Welsh selectors asked their captain, Watcyn Thomas, to play Lemon at prop. Their request was refused which it is thought ultimately cost Thomas his place in the team.

Recognised as probably the best winger in Britain at the time, Ronnie Boon, from the Cardiff club, was also instrumental in the victory, scoring a try and a drop goal. As a Welsh sprint champion over 220 yards, he possessed devastating speed along with evasive skills which made him a difficult man to stop. Allied to these talents was an ardent belief in his own abilities and an unswerving confidence which gave rise to the nickname of 'Cocky'. In that connection it is said that his refrain when arriving in the Cardiff dressing room before a game was always 'Have no fear, Boon is here!'

A native of Barry, he was playing for Dunfermline at the time of the 1932 game, although he was still registered with Cardiff. He had been appointed to teach at the town's high school where he remained until 1938. He also turned out for London Welsh and served as secretary there for several years in the Sixties. He became a HMI and also served on the Sports Council for Wales, before emigrating to New Zealand in 1995, where he passed away three years later.

In the 1932 match his deceptive running bamboozled the English defence to allow him to cross for his country's only try, converted by skipper Bassett, who also kicked a penalty goal. The latter's leadership was inspirational and his play at full-back particularly reliable. He won 15 caps in all and played in five Tests on the British Isles tour of Australia and New Zealand in 1930, when he was described as the best full-back in world rugby.

Boon's final score was perhaps even more mystifying than his run-in for the earlier try. Having initially confused the opposition with a series of sidesteps, he successfully undertook to drop a goal from almost under the English crossbar, a 'spooned' kick which observers described as 'freakish'. Notwithstanding his significant role in the Wales victory, their next game against England a year later saw him make an even more telling contribution.

18

21 January 1933: Twickenham
7–3: Wales won by 1 try and 1 drop goal to 1 try

Wales: V.G. Jenkins (Bridgend), R.W. Boon (Cardiff), E.C. Davey (Swansea), W. Wooller (Rydal School/Colwyn Bay), A.H. Jones (Cardiff); H.M. Bowcott (London Welsh), M.J. Turnbull (Cardiff); E. Jones, B. Evans (Llanelli), A. Skym (Cardiff), R.B. Jones (Cambridge Univ.), D. Thomas (Swansea), T. Arthur (Neath), +W. Thomas (Swansea), I. Isaacs (Cardiff).

England: T.W. Brown (Bristol); L.A. Booth (Headingley), D.W. Burland (Bristol), R.A. Gerrard (Bath), +C.D. Aarvold (Blackheath); W. Elliot (United Services), A. Key (Old Cranleighans); N.L. Evans (Royal Navy), G.G. Gregory (Bristol), R.J. Longland (Northampton), C.S.H. Webb (Devonport Services), A.D.S. Roncoroni (Richmond), A. Vaughan-Jones (United Services), B.H. Black (Blackheath), R. Bolton (Wakefield).

This was Wales's first ever win at Twickenham, in front of a Championship record crowd of 64,000 spectators, after nine unsuccessful visits. It was also the third consecutive game when England had failed to beat the men in red, which was indicative perhaps of a change in the fortunes of the Welsh team following a number of lean years. However this represented their only victory that season and they did not become champions again until 1935. Yet the period in question saw debuts by many promising young players.

This particular game saw the introduction of a new law by the IRB which stated that the first forward to arrive at a stoppage which called for a scrum would be the first man to pack down in that scrum. Such legislation had little support from the home unions who, in recent years, had pioneered the nurturing of players who specialised in particular positions. The IRB considered such a development to be detrimental to the game but within two seasons they were forced to capitulate with regard to that particular ruling.

Almost half the members of the Wales team were winning their first cap on this particular day and the side contained a balanced blend of players from a variety of backgrounds. Skipper Watcyn Thomas expressed some reservations a few years later that the Wales selectors during this period had a predilection for Oxbridge-educated players. In that connection the team contained Jenkins, Bowcott, Turnbull and R.B. Jones who were all of that ilk, and also the 20-year-old Wilf Wooller, who had stayed on at Rydal School in the hope of getting the required grades for entry to Cambridge. In addition, a number of former students from other universities and colleges, such as Boon, Thomas and Davey had been selected.

However, in contrast, the front row contained a former collier, a tin worker and a steelworker. Four of the team, Jenkins, Boon, Wooller and Turnbull represented Glamorgan at cricket, with the latter becoming the first Welshman to play cricket for England. He was truly an all-round sportsman in that he was also selected for Wales at hockey and squash. He was sadly killed by a sniper's bullet during the Normandy fighting of 1944. Wooller could very well have opted to represent England since he was born in Colwyn Bay of English parents. But his fellow centre, Claude Davey, with whom the 6' 2" long-striding Wooller had played at Sale, was determined that his talents should be utilised by Wales.

Throughout the match Watcyn Thomas would speak in Welsh to his front row, who were all natives of Llanelli. However, the usual advantage of confusing the opposition which the team could derive from such a practice was nullified in this particular instance in that the England forward, Arthur Vaughan-Jones, who, as a lieutenant in the Army played for United Services, was a Welsh-speaker from Pontarddulais!

Number 8 Thomas was a highly respected captain and an

imposing figure on the field. His large build of 6' 3" and 15½ stone made him a force to be reckoned with, while his durability was in no doubt, as demonstrated when two years previously against Scotland he played for 70 minutes with a broken collarbone. His sometimes robust style could be considered to be in the tradition of his great uncle, a mountain fighter by the name of Dai Dychrynllyd (Frightful Dai) and Thomas may have served as an inspiration for hooker Bryn Evans, in this 1933 match, who refused to leave the field despite having broken his nose after 15 minutes, which resulted in him bleeding profusely for the rest of the game! It was claimed (but denied by Watcyn Thomas!) that in his dressing-room address before the game in question, he told his players, 'If you see a dark object on the ground, kick it! If it squeals, apologise!'

However, his attributes were not confined to the physical. He was the first Number 8 to captain his country and was described as the Mervyn Davies of his era. He was an excellent tackler, a reliable winner of good ball in the line-out and whose perceptive reading of the game was aided by the fact that, prior to settling for a position in the pack, he had also played in every position behind the scrum except outside-half. By 1929 he'd taken a teaching position at Cowley Grammar School, St Helens, and two seasons later captained Lancashire when they won the English County Championship.

England led 3–0 at half-time, courtesy of a try by Elliot which many observers thought should have been disallowed since he appeared to knock the ball on when in the act of touching down. However, the home team had numerous chances to go further ahead during that first half but loose passing and sterling defence, particularly by full-back Jenkins, who elected to play despite suffering from flu, thwarted their efforts. One of the main instigators of the England attacks was their centre, Don Burland, who initially broke through the attempted tackles of his marker, the inexperienced Wooller, with comparative ease. However, the young Wales centre, having been given prudent on-field advice by skipper Thomas and Davey, soon settled down and successfully adjusted his tackling method to take Burland low and from the side, thus depriving the opposition of one of their most potent attacking ploys.

Wales went into the lead by 4–3 immediately after the restart when Boon fielded a misdirected clearing kick from Gerrard, the England centre, and calmly dropped a goal, although some critics observed that moving the ball to unmarked men outside him might have been more prudent. Whereas the English tactics in the first half had endeavoured to put the rather inexperienced Welsh team under early pressure, the visitors' pack gradually took control after the break. Although they hadn't fared too well in the scrums, the tactic now adopted by skipper Thomas of having Bowcott regularly drive the forwards, who were completely dominant in the line-outs, up the field with a succession of demoralising line-kicks, paid handsome dividends (in those days the team kicking to touch kept possession).

By the middle of the half the English pack had been well-tamed yet, following another Wales attack, an interception by Elliott almost brought him a second try. He set off on a 60-yard sprint for the visitors' line, doggedly pursued by Wooller who, with a desperate try-saving tackle, managed to bring him down with two yards to spare. Yet the score remained unchanged until five minutes from the end when a well-timed pass from Davey enabled Boon to round his marker, Bolton, with ease to touch down. The Englishman was winning his first cap having started the game in his natural position of flanker, but following an injury to one of his team's three-quarters, who had to leave the field, Bolton was faced with the nightmare of having to mark the speedy Boon for the final half-hour!

Jenkins took the conversion and seemed to have made sure of the two extra points to make the score 9–3, which the Twickenham scoreboard duly recorded. However, although the Welsh touch judge had indicated that the kick had gone over, the referee confirmed after the match that he had deemed the kick to have failed. Consequently the official final score was 7–3 to Wales which later surprised many spectators who had been present at the game. As a result of the confusion the IRB moved to introduce a new law the following season which stated that following an unsuccessful conversion the match should restart with a drop-kick as opposed to a place-kick.

19

15 January 1938: Arms Park, Cardiff

14–8: Wales won by 2 tries, 1 conversion and 2 penalty goals to 2 tries and 1 conversion

Wales: V. Jenkins (London Welsh); W.H. Clement (Llanelli), J.I. Rees (Swansea), E.C. Davey (London Welsh), A. Basset; +C. Jones (Cardiff), H. Tanner (Swansea); H. Rees (Cardiff), W. Travers (Newport), M.E. Morgan (Swansea), F.L. Morgan (Llanelli), E. Watkins (Cardiff), A.M. Rees (London Welsh), W. Vickery (Aberavon), A. McCarley (Neath).

England: H.D. Freakes (Harlequins); E.J. Unwin (Rosslyn Park), +P. Cranmer (Moseley), D.E. Nicholson (Harlequins), H.S. Sever (Sale); P.L. Candler (St Barts Hospital), B.C. Gadney (Headingley); R.J. Longland (Northampton), H.B. Toft (Waterloo), H.F. Wheatley, A. Wheatley (Coventry), T.F. Huskisson (OMT), W.H. Weston (Northampton), D.L.K. Milman (Bedford), R. Bolton (Harlequins).

Wales did not register a single victory against England in the four games between 1934 and 1937 and during that period they managed to accumulate just 13 points against them. Perhaps some of the blame could be laid on the fickleness of the Wales selectors, who, for example, for the opening game against England in 1934, selected 13 new caps! This particular encounter in 1938 was the only occasion on which Wales scored as many as 13 points against any country since 1931. These statistics perhaps confirm that during the period in question much greater importance was attached to playing defensive rugby. England in particular were concerned with selecting strong, solid packs which specialised in preventing the opposition from using the ball to any great effect. Wales, on the other hand, still relied upon adventurous three-quarters who unfortunately had to make do with often paltry possession.

On this particular occasion however Wales were clear winners, in front of a crowd of 40,000 and in a gale which was so strong during the singing of the anthems that it had prevented players from standing still. The architect of the home team's victory was fly-half Cliff Jones, considered at the time to be the best in the world in that position. On this particular day he had the luxury of seeing the Welsh pack get the better of their English counterparts. He had first appeared for his country in 1934 having just months previously captained the Llandovery College and Welsh Secondary Schools teams before moving on to get his Blue at Cambridge University.

He had the requirements of the attacking fly-half in abundance, namely electrifying speed (particularly from a standing start), excellent balance facilitated by the low carriage of his 5' 8" and 10 stones 8lbs build, safe hands, a devastating sidestep, a hawk-like eye for an opening, an audacious approach to any defensive challenge and an all-round kicking ability. The essence of his talents in attack was that everything was done at great pace with acute alertness and sagacity, but a criticism sometimes applied to his play was that he did not always know when to pass the ball.

He was, however, the master of a particular attacking ploy which was completely dependant on the timing of his pass. It was usually undertaken in conjunction with Wilf Wooller, from which both Wales, despite a general paucity of possession, and Cardiff reaped ample benefit on many occasions. Having received the ball from his scrum-half, Jones would suddenly accelerate and veer at pace outside his marker as if intending to penetrate the opponents' three-quarter line between the fly-half and the inside-centre. With the latter being enticed to try and stifle the threatened break, Jones would then release the ball to a charging Wooller to take advantage of the resultant temporary breach in the opponents' defensive line and to customarily cause significant damage.

Cliff Jones amusingly attributed many of his skills to being brought up in the densely populated Rhondda Valley, where as a lad he had to learn to dodge and weave on streets full of people, bicycles, lorries and horse-drawn carriages and to avoid the dangers presented by busy tram-lines. However, despite his undoubted agility and resourcefulness, he did not succeed in avoiding entirely the destructive influence of opponents, particularly back-row forwards. For, during his career, albeit a fairly short one, many of his limbs were broken, including his collarbone and both his ankles. Yet he did not wish to see the introduction of rules to curb the activities of fast-breaking, robust flankers, but rather stressed the importance of getting forwards to provide quicker ball for their half-backs and of making half-backs rely on more canny means of avoidance.

Wales, wisely playing to the conditions, took the lead through a try from flanker Alan McCarley, who dribbled from halfway to score. Two penalties from Vivian Jenkins put Wales further ahead and they led 9–3 at the interval. In the second half an astute kick ahead by Cliff Jones led to centre Idwal Rees touching down, with Jenkins adding the conversion. England replied through a try by Sever, converted by Freakes, but in effect they had no answer to the efficacy of the Wales tactics on the day. Both Jones and full-back Jenkins showed their mastery of the art of regularly finding touch in such windy conditions with lengthy kicks of low trajectory to thwart any territorial gains made by their opponents.

Having been one of the two survivors following the 1933 clean sweep, when the selectors chose 13 new caps, the centre, Claude Davey was, on this day, making the last of his seven appearances against England, and winning his 22nd and penultimate cap for his country. Born in Garnant, he played for Swansea, Sale and London Welsh and was one of the most outstanding Welsh three-quarters ever. Renowned for his strong running, bone-shattering tackles and cast-iron hand-offs, he was the Wales midfield powerhouse for many years, using his stocky build to smash uncompromisingly into his opponents which is illustrated, perhaps, by the fact that, in the 1931 fixture with Ireland, he was responsible for knocking both the Irish centres clean out in the tackle. His superhero status was enhanced when he inspirationally led Wales to a 13–12 victory against the 1935 All Blacks, when he also scored a try.

20

15 January 1949: Arms Park, Cardiff

9 3: Wales won by 3 tries to 1 drop goal

Wales: R.F. Trott (Cardiff); K.J. Jones (Newport), J. Matthews, B. Williams, L. Williams (Cardiff); G. Davies (Pontypridd/ Cambridge Univ.), +H. Tanner (Cardiff); E. Coleman, W. Travers (Newport), D. Jones (Swansea), D. Hayward (Newbridge), A. Meredith (Devonport Services), W.R. Cale (Newbridge), J.A. Gwilliam (Cambridge Univ.), G. Evans (Cardiff).

England: W.B. Holmes (Cambridge Univ.); J.A. Gregory (Blackheath), L.B. Cannell, C.B. van Ryneveld (Oxford Univ.), T. Danby (Harlequins), +N.M. Hall (Huddersfield), G. Rimmer (Waterloo); T.W. Price (Cheltenham), A.P. Henderson (Edinburgh Wanderers), M.J. Berridge (Northampton), H.F. Luya (Headingley), G.D'A. Hosking (Devonport Services), E.L. Horsfall (Harlequins), B. Braithwaite-Exley (Headingley), V.G. Roberts (Penryn).

Before a crowd of 51,000 this represented a promising beginning to a very disappointing season for Wales in that it was their only Championship victory. However in coming bottom of the table they conceded only 19 points in their four games. At the close of the previous season England had found themselves at the foot of the table with the result that for this particular match they included nine new caps. One of their debutants was sprint champion Jack Gregory who the previous year, along with the Wales winger on this day, Ken Jones, was a member of the Great Britain team that won a silver medal at the London Olympics in the 4 x 100-metre relay race.

Winning his first of 15 caps for Wales was second row Don Hayward, a railwayman from Newbridge, who from 1951 onwards was regularly selected as prop. He went on to win 15 caps for his country and played in three Tests for the British Lions on their tour of New Zealand and Australia in 1950. Remarkably, winning his ninth cap for Wales in this 1949 fixture, having last appeared for them ten years previously, was the 35-year-old Newport and British Isles hooker, Bunner Travers.

The day before the game the distribution of the Wales team kit for the match was the cause of much consternation. It was found that not only was the team required to wear white shorts for the first time, as opposed to the customary black, but that they were much too long in that the bottoms reached down to the knees. Consequently, a seamstress was hurriedly deployed to make the necessary alterations the night before the game. For future matches the team continued to wear white shorts, except when requested by the BBC to don black shorts in order to assist television viewers to distinguish between teams when watching games in black and white.

With half-backs Glyn Davies and Tanner, who was playing in his seventh and final season of Championship rugby (the first four of which took place before the Second World War) having outstanding matches, England were rarely in the hunt. Fly-half Davies, capitalising on a particularly lengthy pass from his scrum-half partner, constantly breached the English defence with seemingly effortless breaks, two of which led directly to tries by Les Williams. The Cardiff winger (originally from the village of Mynydd-y-Garreg, as was Ray Gravell) still had the task of rounding winger Gregory on both occasions to touch down, and the consequence of the Wales flyer's achievements on the day was that his opposite number was never selected for England again. Later that year, after winning 15 caps, Williams turned to rugby league with the Hunslet club and represented his country in that code also.

When Glyn Davies was first capped for Wales as a teenager in 1947, it was thought that he would make the outside-half position his own for many seasons to come. During the next few years he displayed remarkable talents which made him an extremely attractive player to watch. His running was noted for its grace, poise and deceptive, hip-swaying elegance, and his ability to produce devastatingly smooth sidesteps off either foot made him a very formidable opponent. All of these attributes were displayed with an aura of unflappability which sometimes could give an impression of arrogance. This latter trait was in such contrast to the air of intense effort which emanated from his outstanding successor in the Wales team, Cliff Morgan. Yet in later years it was he who described Glyn Davies as 'probably the most naturally gifted player that I remember at outside-half... he had more fly-half talent in his little finger than any other of his time had in their whole frame... if I wanted to be like anybody it was Glyn.'

Yet Davies's brilliant performances in the red jersey were sometime tempered with indifferent, and sometimes disappointing displays. Neither was he an automatic choice in his position, for the selectors, when closely-fought encounters were anticipated, tended to favour Billy Cleaver at fly-half, whereas if a match involving perhaps more free-flowing rugby was expected, Glyn would be selected. After winning his 11th cap in a particularly bad performance by Wales against Scotland in 1951, which resulted in defeat by 19–0, at the age of 23 years he had played his last game for his country. At the end of his playing career he emigrated to France and became a successful wine trader. He died in Bristol in 1976 at the comparatively young age of 49 years.

Once again, in this 1949 match, the Wales forwards were in control, with John Gwilliam and Alun Meredith in great form, with the latter capping an excellent display with a try. England's only points came from a drop goal by Nim Hall. Ironically, in the corresponding fixture at Cardiff two years earlier, when England won by 9–6, Hall had dropped a goal to earn his side four points. However by 1949 the value of a drop goal had been reduced to three points.

21

21 January 1950: Twickenham

11–5: Wales won by 2 tries, 2 conversion and 1 penalty goal to 1 try and 1 conversion

Wales: B.L. Jones (Devonport Services); K.J. Jones, M.C. Thomas (Newport), J. Matthews (Cardiff), T.J. Brewer (Newport); W.B. Cleaver, W.R. Willis (Cardiff); J.D. Robins (Birkenhead Park), D.M. Davies (Somerset Police), C. Davies (Cardiff), D. Hayward (Newbridge), R. John (Neath), W.R. Cale (Pontypool), +J.A. Gwilliam (Edinburgh Wanderers), R.T. Evans (Newport).

England: M.B. Hofmeyr (Oxford Univ.); J.V. Smith (Cambridge Univ.), B. Boobbyer, L.B. Cannell, I.J. Botting (Oxford Univ.); +I. Preece (Coventry), G. Rimmer (Waterloo); J.M. Kendall-Carpenter (Oxford Univ.), E. Evans (Sale), W.A. Holmes (Nuneaton), G.R.D'A. Hosking (Devonport Services), H.A. Jones (Barnstaple), H.D. Small (Oxford Univ.), D.B. Vaughan (Headingley), J.J. Cain (Waterloo).

Having obtained the Wooden Spoon the previous season the Welsh team, following this encouraging start against England, went on to win the Grand Slam, their first for 39 years. With John Gwilliam as captain for the first time, it was only their second victory at Twickenham in 15 visits, their previous success having occurred in 1933. Their points' aggregate of 50 during this 1950 Championship had only been exceeded once since 1931 (Scotland scored a total of 52 points in 1938), yet Wales's defensive accomplishment was even more notable. They conceded just eight points in their four games, the lowest total in the Championship since 1913, when England completed their season having yielded just four points.

The game was played in front of a record Twickenham crowd in excess of 75,000, which included 20,000 supporters who had made the journey from Wales, and such was the demand for admission to the game that the gates had to be closed one hour before kick-off. England fielded nine new caps on the day, five of whom were Oxbridge students, making a total of seven such students in all, and the fact that their team included three South Africans and one New Zealander led to their being dubbed 'the Foreign Legion', particularly in Welsh circles. The visitors included five players who were representing their country for the first time, including the 18-year-old Lewis Jones, from Gorseinon, at full-back, whose sparkling play was instrumental in gaining the Welsh victory.

He was relatively unknown to the Welsh public, since (although he had signed for Llanelli) his National Service duties entailed that he had played his handful of first-class games up until then in the West Country and normally at centre. He was a little surprised to find that he had been selected to play against England at Twickenham and was concerned to find that he had to make his own way to the ground, since he had no idea where Twickenham was! He later recalled the wording of the letter which officially informed him of his selection. 'You have been selected for Wales versus England at Twickenham on 21 January 1950. Would you make sure that you are at the ground two hours before kick-off. Shirts, shorts and socks will be supplied. Shorts and socks must be returned after the match'!

England scored first when winger J.V. Smith, following an interception some 40 yards from the Welsh line, crashed over in the corner, through Lewis Jones's tackle – a feature of the full-back's play which some critics claimed was his Achilles heel. However his attacking flair more than compensated for any perceived weakness in his defensive armoury. Smith's try was converted by the South African full-back M.B. Hofmeyr. The latter was also an accomplished cricketer for his university and in one game against Gloucestershire he top-scored with an innings of 161. His opening partner on that day, Brian

Boobbyer, who also played for England in this Twickenham match of 1950, was the next highest scorer with 28.

Wales replied eight minutes before half-time following a dazzling piece of Lewis Jones enterprise. He was renowned for pandering to the unexpected and the unorthodox and, when he fielded a stray England kick close to the touchline deep in his own half, instead of settling for the anticipated clearing-kick to touch, he launched a devastating 50-yard run. Having initially thrown a dummy to wrong-foot the advance party of potential English tacklers, he sliced through the opponents' line with a sudden burst of speed on a diagonal, elusive run which took him up to the England 25-yard line. A swift passing movement, involving four players, saw the collier and extremely mobile prop, Cliff Davies, touch down in the corner, giving a half-time score of 5–3.

Early in the second half Jones kicked a penalty goal and then converted a try scored by Ray Cale after a determined dribble by the pack. With the visitors victorious by 11–5, Lewis Jones was carried from the field on the shoulders of delighted Welsh supporters, convinced that a new star had emerged. So it proved to be, although his brief international career, during which he won ten caps, was not sufficient to allow Welsh rugby followers to fully appreciate his prodigious talents.

During his time in the Wales team he earned a reputation as an extremely deceptive and penetrative runner. His versatility was also highly valued in that by the time he had reached 20 years of age, and had won seven caps, he had played in three different positions for his country. As a runner his trademark ploy was a hypnotic change of pace which saw him firstly mesmerise his opponents with a peculiar shuffle of the legs which regularly saw defenders trailing in his wake.

Initially he was one of only two Wales players from the 1950 Championship team to be omitted from the Lions party to visit New Zealand and Australia later that year. However, some six weeks into the tour, the Irish full-back George Norton was injured and Jones was summoned as a replacement. He became the first ever British Isles rugby tourist to be flown to his playing destination when he undertook a four-and-a-half-day journey, involving five plane changes, to New Zealand.

He made an invaluable contribution to the tour, not only through his enterprising play but also his all-round points-scoring ability. Although the tour was halfway through when he arrived, his final tally was 92 points, just six points fewer than the total of the leading scorer, Malcolm Thomas. In the first Test in Australia he accumulated 16 points by scoring in every way possible (a try, two conversions, two penalty goals and a drop goal) and became the first Lions tourist to achieve such a feat.

Having played for Llanelli for two seasons, Jones joined the Leeds Rugby League Club in November 1952 for a fee of £6,000 (a record signing-on fee for any player). Despite not making his mark immediately, he became one of the greatest ever rugby league players. He remained at Leeds for 12 seasons, breaking many records and scoring over 2,000 points and has a stand named after him at the Headingley ground. He played for Wales and Great Britain (15 times), and on the latter's tour of Australasia in 1954 he scored a record-breaking 278 points. He was also selected for The Rest of the World team. He spent six years in Australia as player coach with the Wentworthville club in the Sydney area. Upon his retirement from the game he remained in Leeds and entered the teaching profession.

22

20 January 1951: St Helen's, Swansea

23–5: Wales won by 5 tries and 4 conversions to 1 try and 1 conversion

Wales: G. Williams (Llanelli); K.J. Jones (Newport), J. Matthews (Cardiff), L. Jones, M. Thomas (Devonport Services); G. Davies (Cambridge Univ.), W.R. Willis (Cardiff); J.D. Robins (Birkenhead Park), D.M. Davies (Somerset Police), C. Davies (Cardiff), R. John (Neath), D. Hayward (Newbridge), R.T. Evans (Newport), +J.A. Gwilliam (Edinburgh Wanderers), P. Evans (Llanelli).

England: E.N. Hewitt (Coventry); C.G. Woodruff (Harlequins), L.F.L. Oakley (Bedford), B. Boobbyer (Oxford Univ.), V.R. Tindall (Liverpool Univ.); I. Preece (Coventry), G.R. Rimmer (Waterloo); R.V. Stirling (Leicester), T. Smith (Northampton), W.A. Holmes (Nuneaton), D.T. Wilkins (Roundhay), J.T. Bartlett (Waterloo), +V.G. Roberts (Penryn), P.B.C. Moore (Blackheath), G.C. Rittson-Thomas (Oxford Univ.).

Once again England made wholesale changes for their opening fixture in the 1951 Championship and selected ten new caps. Wales, on the other hand, included 11 players who had been on the previous year's tour to New Zealand with the British Lions and 13 of the 1950 Triple Crown-winning team. Coupled with fact that Wales were seeking their fifth consecutive Championship victory, they were made clear favourites to win this particular match.

The five tries scored by the home team was their second-highest tally against England, following their eight-try haul in 1922. The fact that all the tries were scored by their three-quarters was perhaps an indication of the sparkling play, adeptly orchestrated by Willis and Davies at half-back, which they produced on the day in question. The excellence of the Wales performance, with Dr Jack Matthews and Lewis Jones at their devastating best, was boosted by the innocuous display of the England team, particularly at forward.

This was Matthews's final appearance against England having lined up against them in each of the five matches played between the two countries since 1947. He literally started the game with a bang as he flattened his opposite number, Oakley with a trademark thunderous tackle, thus ensuring that the latter thereafter lost confidence and interest. Matthews had become master of the art of tackling, not only as a defensive necessity but also as an extremely useful attacking option. He was recognised as probably the hardest tackler in international rugby and during the British Lions tour to New Zealand the previous year his performance in that respect earned him the title of 'The Iron Man'. This acolyte was no doubt enhanced by the fact that in the third Test he fractured the breastbone of the home team's skipper, centre Ron Elridge, in a typically ferocious tackle.

Indeed Fred Allen, who had just retired as an All Black player at that time and who went on to become one of the most successful New Zealand coaches ever, described Dr Jack as 'the greatest head-on tackler I ever saw', stating that following a Matthews tackle the next person to arrive ought to be the rag-and-bone collector! As a young lad in the attic of his Bridgend home he had perfected his tackling technique and timing by hurling himself continually against a heavy sandbag. So, aided eventually by his chunky build of 5' 8" and 14 stone 9lbs, when he entered senior rugby in due course he was well prepared to do significant damage. An indication perhaps of his physicality, and of his talents as a boxer, was the fact that while he was a medical student at Cardiff he fought a draw, over three rounds, with Rocky Marciano, a GI who was stationed the St Athan airbase and who some years later retired as undefeated heavyweight champion of the world.

However, on the rugby field his prowess was not confined

to his mastery of the tackle. He was a punishing runner with the ball in hand and able to resort to an explosive turn of speed, as befitted a former Wales 220 yards junior champion, to power his way past opponents. Indeed, having received the ball from Glyn Davies just inside the English half, he clinically exemplified that particular talent, along with the added skill of being able to jink at pace inside would-be tacklers, and gave Wales the lead by crossing near the posts. Lewis Jones kicked the conversion and before half-time the hosts went further ahead when a flowing three-quarter movement saw the ball reach Malcolm Thomas wide out on the left for the winger to cross in the corner, giving Wales a half-time lead of 8–0.

However England hit back with an excellent try early in the second half. Scrum-half Rimmer, having breached the Wales defence on a cross-field run, passed inside to the supporting Rittson-Thomas who cut inside and galloped over from 40 yards for a try, which was converted by Hewitt. Another swift three-quarter movement by Wales saw the ball reach Ken Jones on the right wing on the England 25-yard line. He jinked inside three clutching defenders to cross near the posts. The conversion by Lewis Jones put Wales 13–5 in front and the home team soon extended their score with another typical Matthews try. Lewis Jones, having skilfully glided through the English defensive line, found his fellow centre on his shoulder. Dr Jack took his pass at speed and burst over the line from 30 yards.

Lewis Jones was again instrumental in the movement which led to the final score, when he dispossessed his opposite centre, jinked outside him and, having drawn the England right wing, released Malcolm Thomas on a 60-yard sprint for the line, which saw him run around behind the posts to touch down. Jones's conversion gave a final score of 23–5 which led to much optimism in Welsh rugby circles that another Triple Crown and Grand Slam would be forthcoming in 1951. However, the next game was against Scotland at Murrayfield where Wales were completely outplayed and lost 19–0, in what became known as 'the Murrayfield Massacre'!

23

19 January 1952: Twickenham

8–6: Wales won by 2 tries and 1 conversion to 2 tries

Wales: G. Williams (Llanelli); K. Jones, M.C. Thomas (Newport), A. Thomas (Cardiff), L. Jones (Llanelli); C. Morgan, W.R. Willis (Cardiff); W.O. Williams (Swansea), D.M. Davies (Somerset Police), D. Hayward (Newbridge), R. John, J.R.G. Stephens (Neath), L. Blyth (Swansea), +J.A. Gwilliam (Edinburgh Wanderers), A. Forward (Pontypool).

England: W.G. Hook (Gloucester); J.E. Woodward (Wasps), A.E. Agar (Harlequins), L.B. Cannell (St Mary's Hospital), C.E. Winn (Rosslyn Park); +N.M. Hall (Richmond), G. Rimmer (Waterloo); E. Woodgate (Paignton), E. Evans (Sale), R.V. Stirling (Leicester), J.R.C. Matthews (Harlequins), D.T. Wilkins (United Services), D.F. White (Northampton), J.M. Kendall-Carpenter (Penzance & Newlyn), A.O. Lewis (Bath).

Another bumper crowd of 73,000 at Twickenham, including some 25,000 supporters from Wales, resulted once again in the gates being closed well before kick-off. Consequently many who failed to gain admission, having been reduced to roaming the adjacent streets where they could at least savour a little of the big-match atmosphere, were invited by sympathetic householders into their homes to watch the game on their television sets, which was a new phenomenon to all but a few of the grateful viewers from Wales.

They were obviously unaware of the bitter controversy taking place in the Wales changing room just before the kick-off. Since Bleddyn Williams had withdrawn from the team the previous evening due to influenza, the selectors had asked Dr Jack Matthews on the Friday night to travel to Twickenham the following morning to take his place. While he was preparing to get changed for the game in the away-team dressing room, he was informed by the Wales selectors (who had hastily convened a meeting in the nearby toilet) that he wouldn't after all be required to play and that Bleddyn's position would be taken by the selected reserve, Alun Thomas. An annoyed Jack Matthews informed the selectors that he never wished to play for his country again.

While this victory once again set Wales on the road to another Grand Slam, England went on to defeat Scotland, Ireland and France. In this particular encounter at Twickenham the score at the end reflected a close battle between two very good teams. Indeed, the home team were in command during the earlier part of the game. Lewis Jones, playing this time on the wing for Wales, had to leave the field after 15 minutes with a torn thigh muscle. While he was receiving treatment England capitalised on the disarray in the visitors' defence resulting from Jones's departure and scored two tries. The first was the result of an excellent contribution from Woodward, the bulky but speedy Wasps winger, who exploited the space now available out wide with a strong run before passing inside for Agar to cross for the opening try.

Shortly afterwards Woodward himself crashed over in the corner for a second try, whereupon John Gwilliam, the Wales captain, called Len Blyth from his position as flanker to plug the gap on the wing. Consequently, the Welsh forwards came under greater pressure from their English counterparts, who were now able to harass the Wales half-backs continually. However, when Lewis Jones returned, having been off the field for some 15 minutes, the Welsh pack, with John, Hayward and W.O. Williams in particular making their mark, began to take the initiative.

Shortly before half-time a scintillating break by Cliff Morgan near his own 25-yard line led to him undertaking a defence-splitting scissors with Ken Jones which resulted in the winger

Ken Jones, the scorer of both Welsh tries

sprinting some 40 yards to touch down for a try. Malcolm Thomas was successful with the conversion which meant that Wales went in at half-time trailing by 6–5. However ten minutes into the second half they took the lead with another try from Ken Jones. Although Lewis Jones was by this time but a hobbling passenger, he played a crucial role in that particular score. As the ball was moved along the three-quarter line, a half-dummy from him wrong-footed the England defence to allow Ken Jones to take the ball at speed and cut inside his marker before rounding Hook, the England full-back, to touch down some 20 yards from the posts. A pulsating 30 minutes followed, with Wales holding on to their lead to take their first step towards another Triple Crown and Grand Slam.

This was Cliff Morgan's first of six appearances against England and, despite the fact that he never scored against them, his exciting running meant that he was always a constant threat. His jinking, thrusting style frequently gave the impression that his efforts placed him at bursting point as he sought to penetrate the opposing three-quarter line or to evade the attention of a marauding wing-forward. His endeavours were assisted by his particularly strong, chunky physique and short, sturdy legs that frequently enabled him to bounce out of tackles. Coupled with a devastating burst of speed and a defence-splitting sidestep (a skill which he attributed to having to avoid cow pats when playing briefly as a youngster on a local field!), such qualities made him one of the most dangerous outside-halves in international rugby.

His success also has to be measured in terms of the laws which were in operation at the time, when flankers were allowed to break early from set pieces. As a result, a fly-half frequently took the ball while confronted literally under his nose by a wing-forward (such as Swansea's Clem Thomas, who frequently played in the same Wales team as Cliff) who was intent on his destruction and who, according to Thomas 'had a licence to kill outside-halves'! Yet Cliff's individualism never belied any selfishness in that he was also acclaimed as an excellent distributor of the ball, thus emphasising his basic tenet that 'everyone knows *when* to do things but only the clever fly-half knows *when not* to do things'. The large number of tries scored by three-quarters playing outside him for Cardiff, Wales and the 1952 British Lions bears testimony to that fact. He was the star of that Lions tour to South Africa and was known by the press in that country as 'Morgan the Magnificent', a sobriquet which saw its germination in this thrilling victory at Twickenham.

24

22 January 1955: Arms Park, Cardiff 3–0
Wales won by 1 penalty goal to nil

Wales: A.B. Edwards (London Welsh); K.J. Jones (Newport), +B. Williams, G.T. Wells (Cardiff), T.J. Brewer (London Welsh); C. Morgan (Bective Rangers), W.R. Willis (Cardiff); W.O. Williams (Swansea), B.V. Meredith (Newport), C.C. Meredith, J.R.G. Stephens (Neath), R. Robins (Pontypridd), N.G. Davies (London Welsh), S. Judd (Cardiff), B. Sparks (Neath).

England: +N.M. Hall (Richmond); J.E. Woodward (Wasps), J. Butterfield (Northampton), W.P.C. Davies (Harlequins), R.C. Bazley (Waterloo), D.G.S. Daker (OMT), J.E. Williams (Old Millhillians); G.W. Hastings (Gloucester), N.A. Labuschagne (Guy's Hospital), D.St.G. Hazell (Leicester), P.D. Young (Dublin Wanderers), J.H. Hancock (Newport), P.H. Ryan (Richmond), P.J. Taylor (Northampton), R. Higgins (Liverpool).

Despite, or perhaps because of, the match being postponed for a week owing to 12 inches of snow on the Arms Park pitch, the game was eventually played on a quagmire, before a crowd of 56,000. The atrocious conditions underfoot, along with rain and mist throughout, made for a miserable and forgettable encounter. There were however two notable milestones. Winger Ken Jones was making his 36th consecutive appearance for his country, which was a record at the time. The match also marked the 22nd and last occasion on which Bleddyn Williams, the Cardiff centre, wore the Wales jersey.

He was a master of the sidestep off either foot, but his most telling weapon was the jink. While the former is undertaken at speed the latter is described by the authors of *Fields of Praise* as follows:

Its essence is timing. The jink, Bleddyn's jink, was a more static affair. It meant coming almost to a temporary halt. Its essence was positional and psychological whereby one drew the opponent into knowing the jink was coming, though when it did come he was helpless to do anything about it. The thousands who thronged to see Cardiff play went to see Bleddyn's rippling jink.

He was also a superb passer of the ball with the gift of excellent timing when feeding others, with the result being that he would often take two or three prospective tacklers out of the game by virtue of the precision of his pass. This is borne out by the fact that although he scored numerous tries for club and country, he would regularly present his wingers with a clear path to the line. He was a firm believer in the deceptive merits of carrying the ball before him in both hands. Such a ploy would allow him, while travelling at speed, to lower his shoulder and lean in a particular direction so as to throw any prospective tackler off-balance. His execution of the scissors movement often proved to be an extremely rewarding tactic and in practice sessions he would spend a great deal of time in perfecting this particular skill with fellow players.

He had excelled for Wales for many years with numerous admirable performances yet, on the occasion of this final appearance for his country, he was given no chance, in ankle-deep mud, to display his magnificent talents. Indeed he was of the opinion that the match should not have been played at all in such dire conditions. He had a poor game and suffered the ignominy of being dropped for the next match.

Despite a preponderance of penalty awards in the game there were only two attempts at goal, both by the Wales full-back, Arthur Edwards. One of these produced the only score of the match after ten minutes, when the England forwards had been caught off-side under the posts. Fortunately, a dogged display by the Welsh pack ensured that the visitors were given no real opportunity to counter that score. Edwards had been a late replacement for the selected full-back, Garfield

Owen, who had to withdraw following an accident with some bramble bushes while training with the team at the Glamorgan Wanderers ground.

Wales went on to win the Championship that season by the narrowest of margins. Both they and France had played four matches; both had won three of them and lost the other. The two teams had scored eight tries and conceded three, and both had conceded a total of 28 points in their four games. The crucial difference was that Wales had scored a total of 48 points, while France could only manage 47!

25

21 January 1956: Twickenham

8–3: Wales won by 2 tries and 1 conversion to 1 penalty goal

Wales: G. Owen; K. Jones, H. Morgan, M.C. Thomas (Newport), C.L. Davies; +C. Morgan (Cardiff), D.O. Brace (Newport); W.O. Williams (Swansea), B.V. Meredith (Newport), C.C. Meredith (Neath), R. Robins (Pontypridd), R.H. Williams, (Llanelli), B. Sparks (Neath), L.H. Jenkins (Newport), R.C.C. Thomas (Swansea).

England: D.F. Allison (Coventry); P.H. Thompson (Headingley), J. Butterfield (Northampton), W.P.C. Davies (Harlequins), P.B. Jackson (Coventry); M.J.K. Smith (Oxford Univ.), R.E.G. Jeeps (Northampton); D.L. Sanders (Harlequins), +E. Evans (Sale), C.R. Jacobs (Northampton), R.W.D. Marques (Cambridge Univ.), J.D. Currie, P.G.D. Robbins (Oxford Univ.), A. Ashcroft (Waterloo), V.G. Roberts (Penryn).

In front of a crowd of 75,000, Wales took their first step towards their third successive Championship title and their fifth in seven seasons. Yet in the four games played they amassed a total of only 25 points. They fielded three new caps for this particular match while their opponents had ten newcomers on the field, some of whom were to become renowned in rugby circles all over the world, such as Peter Jackson, the second row pairing of Marques and Currie, and Dickie Jeeps.

One of their debutants, M.J.K. Smith, had a poor game and never represented his country at rugby again, although he played with distinction for the England cricket team in 50 Tests, half of which as a popular captain. His half-back partner in the Oxford University rugby team was Onllwyn Brace, who was also making his international debut for Wales on this day.

He had a reputation as an exciting and enterprising scrum-half, yet rarely had an opportunity to display his particular talents during his nine appearances in the Welsh jersey.

In a scrappy match and on a heavy pitch Wales took the lead after ten minutes when Robins charged over from 20 yards. Garfield Owen kicked the conversion, yet the home team had much of the play due to the dominance of their pack. But their promising work was often undone by careless handling by their backs, with the result that during the first half England failed to capitalise on their territorial superiority despite some probing runs by winger Jackson. They reduced the visitors' lead to 3–5 with a penalty goal by full-back Allison early in the second half, but Wales went further ahead with a try by debutant C.L. 'Cowboy' Davies.

After flanker Brian Sparks had charged down a drop-kick attempt by Mike Smith near the Wales 25-yard line, Malcolm Thomas succeeded, contrary to England full back Allison's vain effort, in picking up the rolling ball to feed Davies on the halfway line. The Cardiff winger threw back his head and sprinted for the line, which he crossed by sliding backwards on his stomach as he just managed to escape the despairing clutches of the covering Mike Smith. England continued to press for the remainder of the game but Wales held out to record their third victory in four visits to Twickenham.

The remarkable front row of W.O. Williams, Bryn Meredith and Courtney Meredith were to play just one more game as a unit following nine appearances together in the Wales jersey. The previous season they had excelled for the British Lions in the drawn series with South Africa when they played in all four Test matches. Their rugged unyielding performance, against formidable opposition in those games, provided an excellent platform for backs such as Cliff Morgan, O'Reilly, Butterfield and Pedlow to work their magic.

The three were also schooled in the merits of psychology when appropriate. During the early Test matches on that tour they were regularly confronted by an opposing front row which took great delight in undertaking non-stop chit-chat in Afrikaans, their native language, in the scrums with a view to undermining the confidence of their Welsh counterparts, who of course had no idea what was being discussed. None of the Lions trio spoke Welsh but knew enough of the language to be able to similarly bamboozle the opposition front row, by the latter part of the series, with the Welsh equivalent of stock phrases such as Good Morning, Good Night, Merry Christmas and Happy New Year!

This was the last and tenth occasion on which the brilliant Wales winger, Ken Jones, faced England having played his first game against them in 1947. Cliff Morgan described his contribution as follows: 'I can't think of any winger I've watched or played with over the years who gave me such a thrill as he moved with the ball. He was electric.' Apart from his incredible speed (he won a gold medal at the 1948 Olympics as a member of the Great Britain 4 x 100 metres relay team and 17 domestic sprint titles) he was an excellent ball-handler with a particular aptitude for making room for his penetrative, graceful runs in sometimes the most confined of spaces.

In 44 appearances for his country, all of which but one were consecutive, he scored 17 tries. For his club, Newport, he scored 145 tries in 293 matches and on the British Lions tour of New Zealand crossed 17 times in 17 matches, including a magnificent try in the fourth Test which was dubbed 'the greatest try of all time' by the New Zealand press.He was also chosen as one of the 'Five Players of the Tour'. Perhaps his greatest claim to rugby fame was scoring the winning try in that rare victory against the All Blacks in Cardiff in 1953. Yet when he was asked which of all the games had given him the greatest pleasure, he replied that he had enjoyed them all and that playing for Wales had been a marvellous experience.

26

17 January 1959: Arms Park, Cardiff

5–0: Wales won by 1 try and 1 conversion to nil

Wales: T. Davies (Llanelli); J. Collins, H. Davies (Aberavon), M. Price (Pontypool), D.I. Bebb (Swansea); C. Ashton (Aberavon), Ll. Williams (Cardiff); R. Prosser (Pontypool), B.V. Meredith (Newport), D.R. Main (London Welsh), I. Ford (Newport), R.H. Williams (Llanelli), +R.C.C. Thomas, J. Faull (Swansea), J. Leleu (London Welsh).

England: J.G.G. Hetherington (Northampton); P.B. Jackson (Coventry), M.S. Phillips (Oxford Univ.), +J. Butterfield (Northampton), P.H. Thompson (Headingley); A.B.W. Risman (Manchester Univ.), S.R. Smith (Richmond); L.H. Webb (Bedford), J.A.S. Wackett (Rosslyn Park), G.J. Bendon (Wasps), J.D. Currie, R.W.D. Marques (Harlequins), A.J. Herbert (Wasps), B.J. Wightman (Moseley), R. Higgins (Liverpool).

On another quagmire of a pitch at the Arms Park the hero of the game was undoubtedly Dewi Bebb, making a fairy-tale debut for his country. The former Friars School, Bangor, pupil, who was a student at Carmarthen Training College at the time, was only the third player from a north Wales schools background to represent Wales, after Wilf Wooller and Bleddyn Williams. Indeed, prior to this match he had played just five games of first-class rugby, with the Royal Navy and Swansea.

Although the state of the pitch prevented both teams from producing any flowing rugby, it allowed the Welsh pack to revel in the conditions. They dominated their opponents but not always by virtue of their abundant possession, for the captain, Clem Thomas, was a firm believer, on wet and muddy occasions, in allowing the opposition to have the ball

101

and to capitalise on the consequent difficulties which they usually faced.

After half an hour the ball was somehow moved along the Wales three-quarter line to Bebb who was tackled by Jackson. In those days the throw-in belonged to the team that was forced into touch and from the resultant line-out, some 15 yards out, the Wales winger threw the ball to R.H. Williams who immediately returned it to him. He, in turn, making light of the heavy ground, swerved inside Jackson and bamboozled Hetherington, the England full-back, with a clinical change of direction. This was the first try scored by any Welsh player against England in Cardiff for ten years. Yet it was a sight to which the England players soon became accustomed, for in his next seven appearances against them Bebb scored five tries. Terry Davies converted his try in the game in question with a fine kick from near the touchline.

This was the start of an illustrious international career for the Swansea player. Winning 34 caps for Wales and becoming one of his country's greatest wingers, he scored 11 tries in all. His forte was electrifying speed which, coupled with a devastating change of pace and an extremely deceptive swerve, made him a difficult opponent to keep in check and gave him a reputation as one of the game's most deadly finishers ever. He represented the British Lions on two tours, playing in eight Test matches. On the second of these tours, to Australia, New Zealand and Canada in 1966, he was joint top scorer with 14 tries.

During the second half of this particular match in Cardiff, as the fervour of the crowd intensified in anticipation of a Wales victory, a number of spectators began to sing 'Hen Wlad fy Nhadau', the Welsh national anthem, which seemed to inspire the team to even greater efforts. It is believed that this was the first time ever for a crowd to break into song during the course of any game in Britain, if not beyond. At the end of the game in their jubilation they carried Bebb shoulder-high from the field.

Dewi Bebb scores the winning try on his debut

In contrast to the debutant winger, someone making his final appearance against England at Cardiff that day was the Llanelli second row, R.H. Williams. After this game he was described in the press 'as a terrible sight to see'! This was a reflection of the vigorous and uncompromising approach that he brought to forward play in general, and to line-out activities in particular, throughout his career. It is ironic perhaps that his fierce reputation as a battling second-row warrior belied a gentle, genial and much-liked disposition, attributes which were also characteristic of Dewi Bebb.

R.H. had made his mark as a forward of international class when he went to South Africa as a member of the British Lions 1955 tour party and played in all four Tests. He was an excellent jumper in the line-out, with a particular ability to fend off the obstructive and destructive efforts of his opponents, and a readiness to let them know, if there was need, that he was disinclined to tolerate any provocation on their part! He applied himself with notable vigour and fire to the scrums and it used to be said that when R.H. hit a maul or a ruck it was usually seen to move backwards.

Yet his reputation became even more celebrated following the next Lions tour in 1959, to Australia and New Zealand. He played in 22 matches in all, including six Tests and was named one of the Five Players of the Year by the discerning *Rugby Almanack of New Zealand*. The legendary All Black second row, Colin Meads, rated R.H. Williams, along with the South African, John Claassens, as the two best second rows he had ever played against.

R.H. captained Wales against England at Twickenham in 1960, when they lost by 14–6, following a disappointing performance. Having been dropped for their next game against Scotland he decided to retire at the end of the 1959–60 season.

27

21 January 1961: Arms Park, Cardiff
6–3: Wales won by 2 tries to 1 try

Wales: +T. Davies (Llanelli); P. Rees (Newport), C. Davies, H.M. Roberts (Cardiff), D. Bebb (Swansea); K. Richards (Bridgend), A. O'Connor; P. Morgan (Aberavon), B. Meredith (Newport), K. Jones, D. Harris (Cardiff), R. Evans (Bridgend), G. Davidge (Newport), D. Nash (Ebbw Vale), H. Morgan (Abertillery).

England: M.N. Gavins (Leicester); J. Young (Harlequins), M. Phillips (Fylde), M. Weston (Richmond), J. Roberts (Old Millhillians), B. Risman (Loughborough Coll.), +R. Jeeps (Northampton); T.P. Wright (Blackheath), S. Hodgson (Durham City), R. Jacobs (Northampton), D. Marques (Harlequins), R. French (St Helens), P. Robbins (Moseley), D. Morgan (Medicals), L.I. Rimmer (Bath).

The three previous encounters between the two countries in Cardiff had produced a total of just 11 points yet although this particular match, too, produced just three scores, the paucity of points belied an entertaining game with an abundance of running rugby despite the heavy conditions underfoot. Eleven of the Wales team hadn't played in the previous season's fixture against England, and for the four Championship games in 1961 Wales were to use 26 players in all.

The highlight of this particular match was the slick running and passing of the Wales three-quarters. The two home tries were the result of such combined play, with Bebb on both occasions completing skilful handling moves with his trademark thrilling dash for the left-hand corner which nonetheless required him to ground the ball securely despite the close attention of his marker. (He also had another try disallowed for foot in touch.) Surprisingly perhaps, Wales led by just six points to nil at half-time, although England contributed to an open game with several promising attacks.

The fluency of the home team backs was in no small way due to the efficient manner in which they were orchestrated by fly-half Ken Richards, who also made three effective half-breaks of his own. However following this, his first Championship match (he had previously been capped six weeks earlier against South Africa, when he also had the distinction of being the first ever Wales outside-half to wear the number 10 on his jersey), there were some who criticised his first-half performance. It was said that he stood too deep behind the scrum, thus preventing him from bringing his three-quarters into play even more frequently.

Richards occupied the outside-half spot for the remainder of the Championship season but then, much to the disappointment of Welsh rugby followers, he joined Salford Rugby League Club in the close season. His home-club followers at Bridgend were to feel the loss even more. Although he had spent some years playing for Swansea and Cardiff it was with the Brewery Field club – which he didn't join until 1960 – that he excelled. There he scored some of the most exciting tries that supporters had ever witnessed. His long-legged physique which gave being to a deceptively loping stride and a telling sidestep, enabled him to breach the most resolute defence. He was also an excellent manager of proceedings on the pitch, a facet which was complemented by his invaluable talents as a kicker, both tactically and as a points' scorer. He was also renowned as a drop-goal specialist who would frequently resort to that method when kicking conversions and penalty goals.

At the end of the 1960–61 season he was the top scorer in Welsh rugby with 289 points. However, while with Salford he had difficulty, on the whole, in adapting to rugby league's defensive systems and his points-scoring record in that particular code was rather nondescript. In 1964 he returned to his native Bridgend and resumed his career as a teacher at Heol Gam Secondary School but in January 1972 he was tragically killed in a road accident at the age of 37 years.

In the second half of this particular match in 1961 Richards had controlled the game admirably, and kicked magnificently in support of his forwards. For after 47 minutes Wales had been reduced to 14 men following the departure of Cyril Davies with a knee injury (which ultimately ended his international career), whereupon flanker Haydn Morgan had to play centre for the remainder of the game, the position which he played when he first joined Abertillery. Yet Wales stood firm in their second-half endeavours until a half-break by the visitors' centre, Phillips, put winger John Young on a path for the try line. The AAA Champion sprinter outflanked the home defence to crash over in the corner, bringing his team to within a single score of their opponents. However, the 14 men, spurred on by the 60,000 crowd's emotional rendition of 'Hen Wlad Fy Nhadau', managed to stem England's final efforts for another dramatic victory.

28

16 January 1965: Arms Park, Cardiff

14–3: Wales won by 3 tries, 1 conversion and 1 drop goal to 1 penalty goal

Wales: T.G. Price (Llanelli); S.J. Watkins, J. Uzzell (Newport), S.J. Dawes (London Welsh), D.I. Bebb (Swansea); D. Watkins (Newport), +D.C.T. Rowlands (Pontypool); D. Williams (Ebbw Vale), N.R. Gale (Llanelli), R. Waldron, B. Thomas (Neath), B. Price (Newport), G.J. Protheroe (Bridgend), A.I. Pask, H.J. Morgan (Abertillery).

England: D. Rutherford (Gloucester); E.L. Rudd (Oxford Univ.) D.W.A. Rosser, G.P. Frankcom (Cambridge Univ.), C.P. Simpson (Harlequins); T.J. Brophy (Liverpool), J.E. Williams (Sale); A.L. Horton (Blackheath), S.B. Richards (Richmond), N.J. Drake-Lee, R. Rowell (Leicester), J.E. Owen (Coventry), N.A. Silk (Harlequins), +D.G. Perry, D.P. Rogers (Bedford).

On another wet, windy and muddy day Wales embarked once again on a Championship-winning trail, against a team that had a three-quarter line of new caps, all of whom had been educated at Oxbridge. The Welsh team also went on to win the Triple Crown for the first time since 1952. Their success that season was achieved in some style in a campaign that was noted for its enterprising rugby, with Wales scoring ten tries in all and, in accumulating 55 points, achieving their highest total since 1931. Yet the key to their victory in this particular game was the fact that their rampaging forwards had dominated the England pack. They were particularly effective in the line-out where they had become masters of double-banking, a ploy which was made illegal later that year when line-outs once again were required to constitute two single parallel lines of players.

With regard to this particular game the Neath prop, Ron Waldron, had waited longer than most to be capped for the first time. For he had initially been chosen to represent Wales in Ireland three years previously but that game was postponed due to an outbreak of smallpox in south Wales. It had taken a long time for him to regain the favour of the selectors! As was the case with regard to Johnny Williams, the England scrum-half who had last played for his country in 1956!

For most of the first half the visitors held their own and trailed at the break by just one drop goal from David Watkins. Wales however took control in the second half and, despite the adverse conditions, played attractive rugby. With Denzil Williams initially making excellent ground, a flowing three-quarter move saw the ball reach Stuart Watkins on the right wing some 30 yards from the line. The long-striding winger outstripped the covering defence to touch down some 15 yards infield. The try was converted by 19-year-old full-back Terry Price who was winning his first cap that day (although he had previously represented Wales against Fiji, when no caps were awarded).

Although England replied with a penalty goal from Rutherford, the home team went further ahead when Haydn Morgan crashed over the visitors' line following a deft kick from his club colleague Alun Pask. The final try, however, has been described as one of the best Wales 'team' tries ever. The movement started when Brian Price won a line-out in the England half. The ball was then transferred through many pairs of hands, involving Denzil Williams, Gale, Thomas, Price again, Rowlands, Dai Watkins, Dawes, Uzzell, and Price again, before Stuart Watkins was given a similar run-in for the line to score his second try.

After the game the England centre Geoff Frankcom claimed that he had been bitten by a Welsh player. No-one owned up to the deed and no individual was censured, but the only member of the victorious team to lose his place for the next game, and for the remainder of the international season, was Brian Thomas!

This was Clive Rowlands's last game against England in what turned out to be his final Championship season. He led Wales magnificently for 13 matches, an honour which was bestowed upon him on the occasion of his first appearance in the red jersey and each time from then onwards that he appeared for his country. He went on to become a distinguished coach and administrator at national and British levels. On the field too he had outstanding leadership qualities and his ability to inspire his fellow players was second to none. He would constantly cajole, exhort and threaten his forwards to greater efforts, while simultaneously smacking his fist into his other hand, with the result that a club colleague playing in the Pontypool pack remarked that Clive had the only cauliflower palm in the game!

He was also a master tactician who could vary his own play as the occasion demanded, and also seek to do so with regard to his fellow players. In that respect his farsightedness as captain was amply illustrated in the next game against Ireland, when, following an injury to Dawes which forced him to leave the field, Clive moved full-back Price to take his place in the centre and then gambled by surprisingly asking Number 8 Alun Pask to play at full-back. In those days it was not a position which was suited to a 6' 3" and 15-stone forward. Yet his captain was aware of Pask's remarkable ball-handling and kicking abilities (this latter skill had been in evidence in the game in question against England, when his tactical kick led to the try by Haydn Morgan).

At the base of the scrum or beside the line-out Clive was an extremely astute operator, with excellent timing with regard to both his runs and his passes. However his forte was his telling tactical kicking, whether in attack or defence. In that respect he gained some notoriety when playing in his second game for Wales against Scotland at Murrayfield in 1963 when, in gaining a Welsh victory by six points to nil, his numerous kicks to touch kept Scotland pinned in their own half for much of the game. Clive, as if to illustrate the extent of his infamy after that occasion, tells an amusing story about his friend, the late Cliff Morgan, coming to play alongside him in a game to celebrate the opening of his local team's new clubhouse in Cwmtwrch. In a memorable speech after the match Cliff thanked his scrum-half for his magnificent service during the game but regretted not having sparkled as he would have liked because, having borrowed Clive's boots for the occasion, every time he wanted to run, his boots decided to kick instead!

29

15 January 1966: Twickenham

11–6: Wales won by 1 try, 1 conversion and 2 penalty goals to 1 try and 1 penalty goal

Wales: T.G. Price (Llanelli); S.J. Watkins (Newport), D.K. Jones (Cardiff), K. Bradshaw, L. Davies (Bridgend); D. Watkins (Newport), A. Lewis (Abertillery); D. Williams (Ebbw Vale), N.R. Gale (Llanelli), D.J. Lloyd (Bridgend), B. Price (Newport), B. Thomas (Neath), G.J. Prothero (Bridgend), +A.E.I. Pask, H.J. Morgan (Abertillery).

England: D. Rutherford (Gloucester); E.L. Rudd (Liverpool), T.G. Arthur, D.W.A. Rosser (Wasps), K.F. Savage (Northampton); T.J. Brophy (Liverpool), J. Spencer (Harlequins); P.E. Judd (Coventry), J.V. Pullin (Bristol), D.L. Powell (Northampton), C.M. Payne (Harlequins), A.M. Davis (Devonport Services), R.B. Taylor (Northampton), D.G. Perry, +D.P. Rogers (Bedford).

A ding-dong battle on a blustery day saw Wales eventually gain superiority and take their first step towards winning the Championship for the third successive season. Despite the fact that England had only beaten Wales once at Twickenham since 1954, Alun Pask became only the fourth Welsh skipper ever to lead his side to victory at HQ.

A penalty from only 20 yards saw Terry Price put the visitors ahead, while a much more difficult penalty kick from the touchline by Rutherford ensured that the teams were on level terms at half-time. The visitors' full-back, with another penalty goal from 35 yards, put Wales 6–3 ahead in the second half, and more enterprising play by the Wales backs brought further rewards. A break by Bradshaw saw him turn back inside and switch the direction of the attack with a pass to D.K. Jones. The Cardiff centre, running across field at speed to outstrip the covering England defence, straightened some five yards from the try line to send Alun Pask diving over in the corner. Price converted with a magnificent kick from the touchline, bringing his tally to eight points, which made a total of 30 points in the five games he had hitherto played for his country (he finished his international career with a total of 45 points in eight matches).

England responded resolutely and got the final score following one of the game's most exciting moves. Rosser, near the halfway line, passed inside to Budge Rogers, who fed Savage. The winger cleverly rounded Stuart Watkins and some five yards from the visitors' line found Perry in support. The Bedford Number 8 crashed over the line to make the score 5–11.

Terry Price, owing to injury, did not play again for Wales that season and only played two more Championship games for his country, against Scotland and France. In July 1967 he joined Bradford Northern Rugby Club, on a four-year contract, at £2,000 per year (a current equivalent value of some £250,000) which was a club record at the time. On his arrival there he would regularly attract some 700 supporters to watch him train and his appearance in home matches invariably meant an increase of 1,500 – 2,000 in the attendance figure. However, there is no doubt that his move to the paid ranks, at the age of 22 years, was a significant loss to Welsh rugby.

From an early age, while still a pupil at Llanelli Grammar School, he had displayed immense talent which had merited his inclusion in the Llanelli team to play Wilson Whineray's 1963–4 touring All Blacks. He had been selected on the left wing but was switched to outside-half early in the second half, a move which was no doubt lamented by Waka Nathan, the celebrated Maori flanker. For in a shuddering, but legal, tackle by Price, Nathan's jaw was broken, an injury which prevented him from playing again on that tour.

The following season Price was capped by Wales and made an instant impression, particularly with his prodigious kicking.

Notwithstanding his achievement as a place-kicker, perhaps the abiding memory for Welsh rugby followers was his 50-yard drop goal in the mud to help clinch the Triple Crown for Wales against Ireland in 1965. Yet his assured, confident style, coupled with significant body strength, often allowed him to engage in enterprising and sometimes adventurous play, to the delight of his followers. His diverse talents led to his selection to tour Australia and New Zealand with the British Lions in 1966, a feat which he repeated with the Great Britain Rugby League team in 1970 when he emerged as the tour's highest scorer with 117 points. He also played rugby league for Wales on five occasions. In 1971 he signed as a place-kicker with the New York-based American football team, Buffalo Bills, but did not turn out for them. In April 1993 he was tragically killed, at the age of 47 years, in a road accident near Oxford, having stopped his car to assist another motorist.

30

15 April 1967: Arms Park, Cardiff

34–21: Wales won by 5 tries, 5 conversions, 2 penalty goals and 1 drop goal to 3 tries and 4 penalty goals

Wales: K.S. Jarrett; S.J. Watkins (Newport), W.H. Raybould (London Welsh), G. Davies (Cardiff), D.I. Bebb (Swansea); +D. Watkins (Newport), G.O. Edwards (Cardiff); D. Williams (Ebbw Vale), N.R. Gale (Llanelli), D.J. Lloyd (Bridgend), B. Price (Newport), G.T. 'Billy' Mainwaring (Aberavon), R. Jones (Coventry), W.D. Morris (Neath), J. Taylor (London Welsh).

England: R.W. Hosen (Bristol); K.F. Savage (Northampton), R.D. Hearn (Bedford), C.W. McFadyean (Moseley), R.E. Webb (Coventry); J.F. Finlan (Moseley), R.D.A. Pickering (Bradford); M.J. Coulman (Moseley), S.B. Richards (Richmond), +P.E. Judd, J. Barton (Coventry), D.E.J. Watt (Bristol), R.B. Taylor (Northampton), D.M. Rollitt (Bristol), D.P. Rogers (Bedford).

It was an encounter known thereafter as 'Keith Jarrett's match' as a result of his remarkable contribution to the result. The 18-year-old debutant scored 19 points, comprising a try, five conversions and two penalty goals. He came close to kicking a third penalty goal, but that hit the post! His achievement equalled a record set by Jack Bancroft in 1910 when Wales defeated France by 49–14. However the result entailed a number of broken records. It was the highest score Wales had achieved since that occasion in 1910, and was also their highest total ever against England. The 21 points scored by the visitors was their highest points haul ever in Wales and the 55 points scored in the game was the highest aggregate ever in games between the two countries.

England, on the back of a convincing win against Scotland,

had come to Cardiff as firm favourites to win the Triple Crown and, for the first time ever against Wales, their team contained no new caps. Wales, on the other hand, had lost all three previous Championship games and were candidates for the Wooden Spoon. During the 1890s Wales had played four matches against England during February (2), December and April. Ever since that period, until this game in 1967, all 56 games between the two countries had been played in January. On this occasion the game had been put back to April to accommodate earlier matches against the touring Australians.

Therefore, on a pleasant spring day with firm conditions underfoot, it was thought that the visitors' attacking talents would prosper. Indeed, following this, their last match of the season, England had accumulated 68 points, the highest Championship total since Wales scored 74 points in 1931. Conversely however, the visitors were runners-up to France in the final table having conceded 67 points, the highest total ever in the Championship by a team finishing in the top two positions. Indeed, in the ten matches played that season 230 points were scored, which was the first time since 1931 that more than 200 points had been scored in the competition.

After leaving Monmouth School at the end of 1966 Jarret had scored 109 points in 16 games at centre for Newport. However, since he had been selected to play at full-back against England, a position where he had never played before, the Welsh selectors had asked his club to play him there against Newbridge the previous Saturday. His performance was so disappointing that skipper David Watkins switched him to his normal centre position for the second half.

It was anticipated therefore that he would be targeted by England and put under pressure with a number of testing kicks. Yet such tactics never materialised, much to the surprise of Jarrett himself, and despite the ascendancy of the visitors' pack, Wales led 14–6 at half-time. However, one of the rare occasions on which he was forced to deal with a high ball served to elevate him to the realms of immortality.

Midway through the second half, with England very much in contention and trailing by just 16–19, Colin McFadyean kicked downfield towards his right-hand touchline. Jarrett had had been instructed by captain David Watkins, who was playing his last match for Wales, to take up a deeper position than was customary. This would enable him to avoid the problem of having to turn towards his own line to retrieve any probing kicks from the England attackers. So, as the Wales full- back prepared to run on to McFadyean's kick, he allowed the ball to bounce before taking it on the burst near the halfway line. He brushed past the challenging Savage to embark on a 50-yard gallop along the touchline to score in the corner, without any interference from his shell-shocked opponents.

Almost every other incident in the game paled into insignificance when measured against the nationwide euphoria and elation that resulted from Jarrett's electrifying contribution. Two tries by Gerald Davies (his first for Wales), following excellent work by firstly Dewi Bebb and then John Taylor, and another by Dai Morris, would have been recalled with greater enthusiasm but for 'that try'! Similarly, too, the record-breaking feat of Roger Hosen, the England full-back, in scoring, with the aid of four conversions in this particular game, a total of 46 points in one international campaign. Also the achievement of John Barton in touching down for two tries, a rare event for a forward in an international match, and Keith Savage in getting the other.

Jarrett's talents were not confined to the rugby field, for he was also a very accomplished cricketer who, like his father before him, represented Glamorgan at first-class level. Indeed later that year he appeared for the county as a middle-order batsman and seam bowler against both the Indian and Pakistani touring sides.

Following the 1967 match against England, he played on nine other occasions for his country in the next two years and also joined the British Lions and Wales on tours to South

Africa and Australia respectively. During this time, using his sturdy 6' and 13-stone build to good effect, he established a reputation as a strong-running, powerful centre and as an accomplished goal-kicker. In one game for Newport against Penarth he set a club record by scoring 30 points. Following the tour to Australia he joined Barrow Rugby League Club for a fee of £14,000, and such was his reputation that he was selected to represent Wales at rugby league before appearing for Barrow for the first time.

Sadly at the age of 25 years he was forced to retire from rugby having suffered a stroke. He had not only illuminated the rugby scene in Wales during his comparatively brief spell but, by virtue of his memorable try against England, had helped to establish the principle of deploying the full-back as an additional attacking force rather than as a purely defensive component of the team.

There is a story, although probably apocryphal, which illustrates the extent of the effect of 'Jarrett's try' on his fellow Welshmen. A bus driver who was returning his vehicle to the depot on the Saturday night of the game saw Keith Jarrett walking along one of Cardiff's streets. He contacted his inspector for permission to use the single-decker bus to run the Wales hero home to Newport, whereupon the official refused, adding 'Leave that bus here and take a double-decker out instead. He might want to smoke!'

31

12 April 1969: Arms Park, Cardiff

30–9: Wales won by 5 tries, 3 conversions, 2 penalty goals and 1 drop goal to 3 penalty goals

Wales: J.P.R. Williams (London Welsh); S.J. Watkins, K.S. Jarrett (Newport), S.J. Dawes (London Welsh), M.C.R. Richards; B. John, +G.O. Edwards (Cardiff); D. Williams (Ebbw Vale), J. Young, D.J. Lloyd (Bridgend), D. Thomas (Llanelli), B. Thomas, W.D. Morris (Neath), M. Davies, J. Taylor (London Welsh).

England: R.B. Hiller (Harlequins); K.C. Plummer (Bristol), J.S. Spencer (Headingley), D.J. Duckham, R.E. Webb (Coventry); J.F. Finlan (Moseley), T.C. Wintle (Northampton); K.E. Fairbrother (Coventry), J.V. Pullin (Bristol), D.L. Powell, P.J. Larter (Northampton), N.E. Horton (Moseley), R.B. Taylor (Northampton), D.M. Rollitt (Bristol), ı D.P. Rogers (Bedford).

With the National Stadium undergoing substantial reconstruction, just 30,000 spectators were allowed to witness this convincing victory which saw Wales win the Triple Crown for the 11th time and the Championship for the 15th time since the inclusion of France in 1910. Two important changes to the laws had been in operation since the beginning of the 1968–9 season. The first was the introduction of replacements for injured players which had earlier that season resulted in Phil Bennett making rugby history. For he became the first player to appear as a replacement in the red jersey of Wales when he took up the position of the injured winger, Gerald Davies, in the game against France. The other change in the laws was the banning of kicks directly to touch between the two 25-yard lines (a rule which the Australian Rugby Union had adopted some years previously). The latter development seemed to have a direct effect on the 1969 Championship matches in that 234 points were scored in total, the highest number since 247 points were scored in 1911. Thirty-two tries were scored in all, with Wales touching down on 14 occasions, the highest Championship total since they crossed for 15 tries in 1931.

During this game the Welsh team certainly revelled in the new obligation to run with the ball, with left-wing Maurice Richards being the main beneficiary as he crossed for a remarkable total of four tries. In so doing he equalled the record set by Willie Llewellyn in 1899 and Reggie Gibbs in 1908. He had already made his mark on the international scene the previous year. His speed, his acceleration from an often static position, and his ability to sidestep with devastating effect off either foot, made him an extremely penetrative runner who was always exciting to watch. His talents had also been recognised by the British Lions and he appeared in three Tests on their tour of South Africa in 1968 as well as playing in 12 provincial matches.

In the game in question against England the dominant home pack had provided a supply of good possession for Gareth Edwards, thus allowing the backs, superbly marshalled by John Dawes, to run smoothly and threateningly for much of the match. The visitors took the lead when Bob Hiller kicked a penalty from directly under the post. This was countered by the home team when Barry John was on hand to pick up in the loose, after Stuart Watkins had been brought down 15 yards from the England line, and feed Richards who touched down unopposed to make the score 3–3 at half-time.

The winger's second try was the result of deft handling by the Wales three-quarters which put him clear in the corner, as was the case with his final try when he lined up to receive the ball between the two centres. His third had followed a blistering run through the middle by J.P.R. Williams, whose frequent incursions into the line played havoc with the visitors' defence. The full-back was brought down just short of the line but was able to transfer the ball to Richards who crashed over.

However the highlight of the afternoon for many was the

second Welsh try scored by Barry John, to make the score 14–3. It was the result of a brilliant solo run whereby, midway between the halfway line and the England 25-yard line and with a move which he constantly practised, he kicked the ball over the heads of the visitors' three-quarters to regather it following a remarkable change of pace to ensure that the bounce was favourable. He then shimmied his way past groping defenders to touch down for one of his best tries in a Wales jersey. He described his progress to the line as going on 'a zigzag run checking one way to go past one opponent, sidestepping the other way to get around another, dropping a shoulder next. Done at pace, soon I was over in the corner.' John Dawes later claimed that he had been fooled three times during that run into thinking that Barry was going to pass to him. In the press the following day the score was described as poetry in motion which should also be put to music!

On the day Barry John also dropped a goal and Jarrett kicked two penalty goals and three conversions, while Hiller replied with three consolation penalties for the visitors. Richards never appeared in another Championship match for Wales. Following the Wales tour to New Zealand and Australia in 1969 he retired from rugby union, having scored 97 tries for Cardiff and seven for his country for whom he played on nine occasions. He saved his most memorable try for Wales until last, when in the second Test against the All Blacks he mesmerised Kirton and McCormick to score what was described at the time as one of the best tries scored at Eden Park for many years.

On his return from that tour he turned to rugby league and signed for Salford for £7,000, but, as a dedicated Christian and lay preacher, he insisted on including a clause in his contract which excused him from playing on a Sunday. In his 14 years with the club, during which he played in a record-breaking 498 matches, he was one of their star performers, scoring a total of 956 points and becoming their top try scorer ever. He also played rugby league for Wales and Great Britain.

32

28 February 1970: Twickenham

17–13: Wales won by 4 tries, 1 conversion and 1 drop goal to 2 tries, 2 conversions and 1 penalty goal

Wales: J.P.R. Williams (London Welsh); S.J. Watkins (Cardiff), W.H. Raybould (Newport), S.J. Dawes (London Welsh), I. Hall (Aberavon); B. John, +G.O. Edwards (Cardiff); D. Williams (Ebbw Vale), J. Young (Harrogate), D.B. Llewelyn (Newport), D. Thomas (Llanelli), T.G. Evans (London Welsh), W.D. Morris (Neath), M. Davies (London Welsh), D. Hughes (Newbridge).

Replacement: R. Hopkins (Maesteg) for Edwards.

England: +R.B. Hiller; M.J. Novak (Harlequins), J. Spencer (Headingly), D.J. Duckham (Coventry), P.M. Hale (Moseley); I.R. Shackleton (Harrogate), N.C. Starmer-Smith (Harlequins); C.B. Stevens (Penzance-Newlyn), J.V. Pullin (Bristol), K.E. Fairbrother (Coventry), A.M. Davis (Harlequins), P.J. Larter, R.B. Taylor, B.R. West (Northampton), A.L. Bucknall (Richmond).

If Wales needed inspiration to rise to the occasion for this game it was provided by Keith Fairbrother, the England tight-head prop on the day, whose comments before the game were reported as follows in the press that morning:

> I hate those bad-losing Welsh. I respect the Welsh for their playing ability and hardness. But I HATE them and can't stand to lose against them. Welshmen are bad losers. If they win they gloat. If they lose they moan. I don't think we rub it in enough when we win.

Cannily, the Welsh coach, Clive Rowlands, pinned the derogatory comments on the dressing room wall.

However, for the earlier part of the match they had no positive effect on the visitors' performance, for England were the superior team and with 20 minutes to go they were comfortably ahead. With their three-quarters moving smoothly and threateningly, particularly in midfield, they scored an early try by Duckham, following great handling from the backs, which was converted by Hiller. Wales replied with a try by Mervyn Davies after he had won possession at the back of a line-out near the England line and crashed over. However the home backs were in rampant mood and Novak crossed, this time in the right-hand corner, after another sparkling move. (The winger's achievement was all the more notable in that he had already played for his club, Harlequins, earlier that day but was called to play at Twickenham as a late replacement for the injured Keith Fielding.) Hiller added the conversion and also kicked a penalty goal to give a half time score of 13–3.

Just before half-time, following a collision with Wales skipper Gareth Edwards, the referee, Robert Calmet, was forced to leave the field with what turned out to be a broken bone in his left leg and a dislocated shoulder. He was replaced by touch-judge Johnny Johnson. The visitors reduced the arrears when an attacking kick by Edwards caused confusion for the opponents' defence and, as the ball rolled over the try line, Barry John was on hand to touch down. However with 20 minutes of the match remaining, Edwards himself had to leave the field. While endeavouring to tackle his opposite number, Starmer-Smith, he suffered a painful injury when Dennis Hughes fell on his ankle. The introduction of Ray 'Chico' Hopkins as a replacement, the first one ever in games between the two countries, brought about an immediate improvement in the visitors' fortunes.

From a scrum near the England line he had intended to move the ball left to Barry John in the centre of the field, but an untidy heel forced him go on the blind side. As he moved towards the touchline, J.P.R. Williams came charging up on his outside to crash over for a dramatic try, his first for his country, making him, along with Vivian Jenkins and Keith Jarrett, only the third full-back to have scored a try for Wales.

Shortly afterwards, following a long and erratic throw by England at a line-out near their goal-line, Hopkins grabbed the loose ball and dived over to score. For the first time ever therefore Wales had scored four tries at Twickenham. Until that last try the goal-kicking duties had been shared by Edwards and J.P.R. (although Barry John, during the latter part of the following season, was chosen to take kicks from positions to the right of the posts, he did not become an established goal-kicker for Wales until after his return from the 1971 Lions tour) but between them they had missed three penalty goals and three conversions. It was with great relief therefore that J.P.R. saw his conversion put Wales in the lead, by 14–13, with very little time remaining. However, with just a minute to go, John casually dropped a goal from 40 yards to seal the victory, an achievement which neither team had previously accomplished when having been in arrears by ten points.

Despite Hopkins's stirring first appearance in the red jersey of Wales it proved to be the only occasion when he represented his country. He was however chosen to tour Australia and New Zealand with the British Lions the following year, where he once again produced some sterling performances in the ten provincial matches in which he played. He also gave a very commendable account of himself in the crucial, victorious first Test against the All Blacks when he played for all but seven minutes of the game following an injury to Gareth Edwards.

On a social level his infectious humour made him one of the most popular members of the touring party. Some of his witticisms have become entrenched in Lions folklore such as his description of Gareth Edwards's prodigious pass: '[H]e passes the ball further than I go on my 'olidays!' As a member of the Llanelli team that beat the All Blacks on 31 October 1972, he had the rare distinction of being victorious against them on two occasions while representing two different teams. Some three months after that historic win at Stradey 'Chico' joined Swinton Rugby League Club.

33

16 January 1971: Arms Park, Cardiff

22–6: Wales won by 3 tries, 2 conversions, 2 drop goals and 1 penalty goal to 1 try and 1 penalty goal

Wales: J.P.R. Williams; G. Davies, +S.J. Dawes (London Welsh), A. Lewis (Ebbw Vale), J.C. Bevan; B. John, G.O. Edwards (Cardiff); D. Williams (Ebbw Vale), J. Young (Harrogate), D.B. Llewelyn, D. Thomas (Llanelli), M.G. Roberts, J. Taylor, M. Davies (London Welsh), W.D. Morris (Neath).

England: P.A. Rossborough (Coventry); J.P. Janion (Bedford), C.S. Wardlow (Northampton), J.S. Spencer (Headingley), D.J. Duckham (Coventry); I.D. Wright (Northampton), J.J. Page (Bedford); D.L. Powell (Northampton), J.V. Pullin (Bristol), K.E. Fairbrother, B.F. Ninnes (Coventry), P.J. Larter (Northampton), +A.L. Bucknall (Richmond), R.C. Hannaford (Bristol), A. Neary (Broughton Park).

Wales, playing at a newly-renovated Cardiff Arms Park, were now entering another 'golden' era. They virtually demolished their opponents to take their first step towards the Grand Slam, their first since 1952. Remarkably, during the international season, they called on just 16 players, and for this particular match they were drawn from only six clubs. England had chosen eight new caps for this opening fixture, whereas Wales had just two debutants. The result meant that the home team, with regard to the annual contest with England, had now won more games than their opponents from across the border. It was the first time since 1912 that they had been in the lead, and that by 33–32.

The superiority of the Welsh team was based on an extremely powerful display by the forwards who completely dominated the opposing pack. Consequently, there was ample opportunity for their enterprising backs to work their magic. Yet it was England who opened the scoring with a try by Hannaford. A collision between Mervyn Davies and Taylor at the back of a line-out enabled the Bristol Number 8 to touch down. John opened the scoring for Wales with a drop goal and closed their account in the same manner in the second half. In three consecutive games against England, therefore, Barry John had kicked four drop goals.

It was 'a first' for most of the other Wales scorers, on many counts. John Bevan, got his first try for his country, Gerald Davies scored his first as a winger and John Taylor, in his newly-deputed capacity as place-kicker from a position to the right of the posts, kicked his first points for Wales with two conversions. He was, of course, in the next match, to etch his name in the annals of Championship drama with a remarkable touchline conversion at Murrayfield, two minutes from the end, to win the game for Wales by 19–18.

Despite the try by Hannaford and a penalty goal by Rossborough the home team gradually took control and were comfortably ahead at the interval by 16–6. As well as assuming mastery in the tight they established in addition profitable ploys in the loose. For example, in the words of Gareth Edwards:

> We all knew about Rossborough, the Coventry full-back. He was rather 'delicate' under the high ball, so we let him have it. We practised long and hard beforehand, Barry and I kicking, Arthur Lewis smashing in on the catcher and John Dawes lurking in a support position to pick up the pieces. Gerald Davies actually scored from this situation.

The remaining Wales points were acquired through another try by Davies and a conversion by J.P.R. In fact it was remarkable that the full-back was still on the field, since after just five minutes of the game he'd suffered a depressed fracture of the cheek-bone in a collision with Gareth Edwards. He was operated on in London to repair the damage, but not until the following week!

John Bevan in his three encounters with England scored three tries but perhaps his greatest achievement was as a member of the 1971 British Lions party that toured Australia and New Zealand. He touched down for 17 tries to equal the try-scoring record on a Lions tour set by the legendary Irish winger Tony O'Reilly. He was a player who preferred to run through defenders, often deploying a powerful hand-off to very good effect, as opposed to running around them, or resorting to a sidestep or a chip ahead. His muscular 6' 0" and 13-stone frame exuded power and aggression and, coupled with a dogged determination and persistence, his fearless style would often cause panic amongst the opposition. When required he could also cover ground with considerable speed and took great delight in harrying opponents when they were in possession.

During training sessions with the Lions in New Zealand he was required on occasions to join the forwards in their allotted tasks, whereupon the coaching staff came to the conclusion that he was stronger than half the Lions forwards! His style of play was ideally suited to rugby league and in 1973 he joined Warrington. In his first game against Castleford he charged over the line from some 20 yards out, with three defenders on his back, to score the first of 200 tries for 'The Wire'.

He later represented Wales and Great Britain at rugby league and the fact that he also played flanker for the former and second row for the latter was further testimony of his strength and mobility. As a member of the Great Britain squad to tour Australia and New Zealand in 1975, he scored 15 tries in 17 games including three tries in the Test series against the Kiwis. Upon his retirement, having served the WRU in coaching capacities for many years, he joined the staff at Monmouth School as a teacher of Religious Education and Director of Rugby Coaching.

34

15 January 1972: Twickenham

12–3: Wales won by 1 try, 1 conversion and 2 penalty goals to 1 penalty goal

Wales: J.P.R. Williams; G. Davies (London Welsh), R. Bergiers (Llanelli), A. Lewis (Ebbw Vale), J. Bevan; B. John; G. Edwards (Cardiff); +D.J. Lloyd (Bridgend), J. Young (Harrogate), D.B. Llewelyn, D. Thomas (Llanelli), T.G. Evans, J. Taylor, M. Davies (London Welsh), W.D. Morris (Neath).

England: +R. Hiller (Harlequins), J.P. Janion (Bedford), M.C. Beese (Liverpool), D.J. Duckham (Coventry), K.J. Fielding (Moseley); A.G.B. Old (Middlesbrough), J.G. Webster (Moseley); C.B. Stevens (Harlequins), J.V. Pullin (Bristol), M.A. Burton, A. Brinn (Gloucester), C.W. Ralston (Richmond), P.J. Dixon (Harlequins), A.G. Ripley (Rosslyn Park), A. Neary (Broughton Park).

England were seeking their first success at Twickenham against Wales since 1960, yet the nine points difference between the two teams at the end represented Wales's biggest away victory margin since they won by 28–18 at Bristol in 1908. The game was played before a sell-out crowd of over 71,000, including some 16,000 from Wales, with many thousands of would-be spectators having their applications for tickets rejected and their money refunded. England had once again rung the changes with eight new caps, whereas Wales included just one debutant, Roy Bergiers.

In a dour game Wales were fortunate at half-time to be ahead by two penalty goals from John to one penalty from Hiller. They had been under pressure for considerable periods during the match; perhaps the fact that John Pullin took eight strikes against the head was an indication of the home team's dominance in the scrum. Yet, as the author Huw Richards notes, the England hooker was dismissive of the Twickenham crowd's appreciation of his achievement in that respect:

> Ninety per cent of the people were there because it was Twickenham. They were not really there to watch the rugby, whereas in Wales it was ninety per cent the other way. If you took one against the head at Cardiff Arms Park, a big noise would go up from the crowd because they understood and appreciated what was happening. If you took one against the head at Twickenham, nobody would know. They wouldn't have a clue what was happening.

The fortunes of the Welsh team improved in the second half and England made comparatively few forays into the visitors' territory. Yet many of the attacking moves produced by Wales were stifled by resolute defence from Duckham and his fellow three-quarters, until J.P.R. made history. At a scrum some 30 yards from the England line, with Barry John lining up to receive the ball from his scrum-half as if to drop a goal, J.P.R. came charging through on the blind side to take the ball on the burst from Edwards. Despite a valiant effort to tackle him by Dixon, a determined dive for the line saw the full-back ground the ball for the first ever four-point try for Wales.

Barry John converted and from then on until the end of the game the Welsh team were in control. They won their next two games against Scotland and France but then, like Scotland, declined the chance for another Grand Slam by refusing to go to Dublin to play Ireland because of escalating violence in Ulster. It was a decision that was much denigrated by the rugby authorities in Ireland, for the cancellation of games against two of the home countries constituted a severe loss of income for the Irish Rugby Union. Ireland too were irked that they also had been deprived of an opportunity to win the Grand Slam, since they were victorious in their away games against England and France.

Barry John did not play against England again, since he

J.P.R. Williams, who in 11 appearances against England, was always on the winning side
© Getty Images

retired at the end of the season (as indeed John Dawes had done in 1971). Perhaps an indication of the pressure that brought him to make such a decision was the fact that at the end of this game Eamonn Andrews stood on the touchline with his red book, ready to whisk members of the Wales team away to Teddington Television Studios to film an episode of *This is Your Life* with their celebrated fly-half. On his retirement he was offered £120,000 to play rugby for South California in the USA. It was a deal brokered by his good friend, the actor Stanley Baker, which he had to turn down because of other commitments, as indeed was the offer to play American football as purely a goal-kicker.

His remarkable achievements as a member of the British Lions party in New Zealand in 1971, and the resultant fame, had led on his return home to countless demands for his presence. He was constantly bombarded with invitations to receptions, award ceremonies, opening ceremonies, dinners and charity events. Sack-loads of letters asking for his autograph would arrive every day, while some autograph hunters would even knock on his door. In due course he began to feel uncomfortable with this celebrity status that had been bestowed upon him. In addition he was of the opinion that such demands were compromising the standards that he had set for himself as a player, and that as a result he was no longer getting the same pleasure from playing. After much soul-searching he decided to retire from the game at the age of 27 years and undertook a career in journalism.

In the opinion of many rugby pundits he remains the best outside-half ever. He accomplished feats on the field which no other player was equipped to emulate and which would leave opponents and spectators alike wondering how on earth such play had been at all possible. He appeared to defy the limitations of time and space, often assuming an apparitional aura as he ghosted his way through a seemingly impenetrable defence or through gaps that were visible to nobody else. Many a bewildered opponent left in his wake would often be reminded of a slogan so frequently applied to magicians: 'Now you see him, now you don't!'

Carwyn James was firmly of the opinion that sporting prowess could sometimes transcend the confines of rules, fitness, coaching and technical excellence to such an extent that, in its pursuit by certain individuals who were inclined to yield to their instinctive nature, it sometimes became an art form. On the rugby field Barry John was the epitome of that theory.

35

20 January 1973: Arms Park, Cardiff

25–9: Wales won by 5 tries, 1 conversion and 1 penalty goal to 2 penalty goals and 1 drop goal

Wales: J.P.R. Williams; G. Davies (London Welsh), +A. Lewis (Ebbw Vale), R.T. Bergiers (Llanelli), J.C. Bevan (Cardiff); P. Bennett (Llanelli), G.O. Edwards (Cardiff); G. Shaw (Neath), J. Young (London Welsh), D.J. Lloyd (Bridgend), D. Thomas, D.L. Quinnell (Llanelli), W.D. Morris (Neath), M. Davies (Swansea), J. Taylor (London Welsh).

England: S.A. Doble (Moseley); A.J. Morley (Bristol), P.J. Warfield (Rosslyn Park), P.S. Preece, D.J. Duckham (Coventry); A.R. Cowman (Coventry, J.G. Webster (Moseley); C.B. Stevens (Penzance-Newlyn), +J.V. Pullin (Bristol), F.E. Cotton (Loughborough Colleges), P.J. Larter (Northampton), C.W. Ralston (Richmond), A. Neary (Broughton Park), A.G. Ripley (Rosslyn Park), A. Watkins (Gloucester).

Replacement: G.W. Evans (Coventry) for Warfield.

This was a season that proved to be unique in the history of the Championship in that each of the five countries won both their home games and lost their two matches away from home, with the result that all five teams finished level on points. Scotland were however deemed champions by virtue of the fact that they scored more points than any of the other teams and despite their conceding more points than they had scored!

England came to Cardiff very much as underdogs in that they had lost their four previous encounters against Wales, who were looking for their ninth consecutive victory in the Championship whereas England had been defeated in their last five matches. Indeed the prognostications of Welsh success were correct and in this match, for the third time in four visits, their opponents conceded five tries.

The England forwards were completely outplayed by the home pack and whereas the scintillating running and passing of the Wales three-quarters was facilitated by an abundance of possession, it was also assisted at times by the poor quality of the visitors' play. Clem Thomas, writing in *The Observer*, gave an illustration of such ineptitude. 'On one occasion, and all at the same time, Sam Doble missed a kick ahead, managed to scramble possession, ran into his own man and then kicked the ball into Welsh hands to set up a Welsh counterattack.'

Yet with the score at just 12–6 at the interval, following tries by Bevan, Gerald Davies (who scored as Evans, the England centre, was waiting to take the field in place of the injured Warfield), and Gareth Edwards, England were still in contention. Indeed Wales did not put the result beyond doubt until injury time, when tries by skipper Arthur Lewis and a second by John Bevan sealed the victory. A drop goal by Cowman and two penalty goals by Doble accounted for the England total.

Lewis, on this the occasion of his eighth cap, was the first player from the Ebbw Vale club to captain his country. He won 11 international caps in all, but was of the opinion that he could well have won more had he played for a more fashionable club. He was finally recognised by the Welsh selectors at the comparatively late age of 28 years, despite having had a very successful career at club level. As a schoolboy playing local representative rugby he was the preferred choice at outside-half at the expense of David Watkins who was obliged instead to play at scrum-half.

In 1971 Lewis made a significant contribution to the success of the British Lions tour to Australia and New Zealand and represented the team in ten provincial matches. Weighing over 12½ stone and standing 5' 10" tall, his sturdy build gave him a formidable presence in the centre. His charging penetrative runs would see him burst through the most resolute defence while his tackling was of the highest order. Perhaps his greatest quality was his excellent distribution, allowing those outside him to benefit from more time and space as provided by the skilful timing of his passes. In that respect he assumed the mantle of John Dawes, following the retirement of the former Wales and Lions captain.

36

15 February 1975: Arms Park, Cardiff

20–4: Wales won by 3 tries, 1 conversion and 2 penalty goals to 1 try

Wales: J.P.R. Williams (London Welsh); G. Davies (Cardiff), S.P. Fenwick (Bridgend), R. Gravell, J.J. Williams (Llanelli); J.D. Bevan (Aberavon), G.O. Edwards (Cardiff); A.G. Faulkner, R.W. Windsor, G. Price (Pontypool), A.J. Martin (Aberavon), G. Wheel, T.P. Evans, +M. Davies (Swansea), T.J. Cobner (Pontypool).

Replacement: D.L. Quinnell (Llanelli) for Wheel.

England: A.M. Jorden (Bedford); P.J. Squires (Harrogate), K. Smith (Roundhay), P.S. Preece, D.J. Duckham (Coventry); M.J. Cooper, J.G. Webster (Moseley); C.B. Stevens (Penzance-Newlyn), P.J. Wheeler (Leicester), +F.E. Cotton (Coventry), N.E. Horton (Moseley), C.W. Ralston (Richmond), J.A. Watkins (Gloucester), R.M. Uttley (Gosforth), A. Neary (Broughton Park).

Replacements: S. Smith (Sale) for Webster; J.V. Pullin (Bristol) for Wheeler.

For the third successive time at Cardiff, Wales scored 20 points or more against England, as they accumulated – mainly as a result of the 32 points scored against Ireland a month later – their highest points' total (87) in the Championship since 1910. An unexpected defeat against Scotland denied them the Grand Slam but they finished the season as champions. Remarkably, neither team on this day in Cardiff included players who were making their first appearance for their country. Yet, after a period of transition, the 1975 international season saw the cementation of several influential Championship partnerships, such as Gravell and Fenwick in the centre, Martin and Wheel in the second row and the legendary 'Pontypool front row'.

Mervyn Davies, the Wales Number 8, was leading his country for the second time, a role which he assumed with great success. Until his premature retirement from the game, as the result of a brain haemorrhage tragically suffered while playing for Swansea in March 1976, he had captained Wales on eight occasions, during which time they were defeated in only one game. Such a record saw him being voted, in 2002, the greatest ever Welsh captain, in a poll of rugby followers organised by the Welsh press on the occasion of the inauguration of the Welsh Rugby Former International Players Association. In that poll he was also voted the best ever Wales Number 8 and at the time of his retirement was generally considered to be the best Number 8 in the world.

Wales started the game strongly and efficiently and succeeded in continuously denying England the opportunity to form an attacking platform despite the visitors obtaining an adequate supply of possession. Indeed their three-quarters failed to threaten the Wales defence until well into the second half. At the interval Wales led by 16–0 and appeared to be coasting. Both J.J. Williams and Gerald Davies had scored tries resulting from characteristic, crashing breaks by Ray Gravell. This was only his second appearance in a Wales jersey and his reputation for forceful direct running, complemented by a ferocious hand-off, powerful acceleration and an ability to put his wingers into space, was already taking hold.

The Wales total at half-time also comprised a conversion and two penalty goals by second-row Allan Martin. Recognised primarily as a majestic line-out jumper he was occasionally, during his 34-cap tenure in the Wales team, called upon to undertake goal-kicking duties, particularly long-distance attempts. In all he accumulated 21 points for his country in that capacity.

However, in the second half the home pack was no longer dominant and the team's initial fluidity was now lacking. They seemed prepared to rest on their laurels until a 74th-minute try by the England second row, Nigel Horton, galvanised them into greater efforts and a sparkling handling movement saw Steve Fenwick touch down for the final try. But even better things were to come the following season.

37

17 January 1976: Twickenham

21–9: Wales won by 3 tries, 3 conversions and 1 penalty goal to 3 penalty goals

Wales: J.P.R. Williams (London Welsh); G. Davies (Cardiff), R. Gravell (Llanelli), S.P. Fenwick (Bridgend), J.J. Williams; P. Bennett (Llanelli), G.O. Edwards (Cardiff); A.G. Faulkner, R.W. Windsor, G. Price (Pontypool), G. Wheel (Swansea), A.J. Martin (Aberavon), T.J. Cobner (Pontypool), +M. Davies, T. Evans (Swansea).

England. A.J. Hignell (Cambridge Univ.); P.J. Squires (Harrogate), A.W. Maxwell (Headingley), D.A. Cooke (Harlequins), D.J. Duckham (Coventry); M.J. Cooper (Moseley), M.S. Lampkowski (Headingley); F.E. Cotton (Sale), P.J. Wheeler (Leicester), M.A. Burton (Gloucester), W.B. Beaumont (Fylde), R.M. Wilkinson (Bedford), M. Keyworth (Swansea), A.G. Ripley (Rosslyn Park), +A. Neary (Broughton Park).

Replacement: P.S. Preece (Coventry) for Squires.

This was Wales's highest total on English soil since they defeated England by 28 points to 18 at Bristol in 1908, and their highest score ever at Twickenham. This was their first victory en route to winning another Grand Slam and in so doing scored 102 points, the biggest ever aggregate in the history of the Championship. England, on the other hand, for the third successive season, went on to claim the Wooden Spoon, and with this particular match began a sequence of five games without registering a single try against Wales. Remarkably, all the Swansea back row had been selected, with two playing in the red of Wales and one representing England.

It was a particularly noteworthy occasion for J.P.R. Williams in that he exceeded Billy Bancroft's total of 33 appearances for his country to become Wales's most capped full-back. He also scored two tries, which brought his total to four against England, to which he added another the following season at the Arms Park. In all he made 11 appearances against them and had the admirable record of never having been on the losing side.

Despite the fact that the Welsh performance in some respects was disappointing, J.P.R. was at his marauding best both in defence and attack. A week before the game, when playing for London Welsh, he had received eight stitches in a cut over his right eye. This time, at Twickenham, blood poured from a gash under his left eye and despite being given stitches after the game he continued to bleed for hours afterwards! Fortunately expert medical assistance was usually at hand to treat such injuries during a match but J.P.R. was even known, on one occasion, to have stitched his own eye-wound during half-time!

Many critics, pundits and fellow players have commented on his durability. According to Gerald Davies his commitment 'bordered on the frightening'! Carwyn James described J.P.R. as being like a forest animal blessed with the sixth sense for the presence of danger, an element which he often sought and loved. To John Dawes he was brave, committed and totally uncompromising. According to Tim Glover, writing in *The Independent*, 'no doctor has ever played rugby with such total disregard for his own well-being since J.P.R, complete with bloodied headband, was charging around Cardiff Arms Park like a wounded bison'!

The opening exchanges of this particular encounter were fairly even until midway through the first half. Then Gareth Edwards, who was also having an excellent game, capitalised on a misunderstanding between Ripley and Lampkowski at the base of a scrum near the England line to touch down. This was followed by the first of J.P.R.'s tries. Once again, from a scrum five yards from their opponents' line, the visiting three-quarters worked their magic. Quick ball from Mervyn Davies saw Edwards pass to Bennett who, having missed out Lewis, passed to Fenwick. He in turn, over the head of the supporting J.P.R., floated a rather high pass to J.J. Williams. He gathered with a little difficulty and, before being collared, threw an overhead pass to J.P.R. who was now storming through on his inside. The full-back took the ball at pace some 20 yards out, charged through two tackles from England defenders and scored near the corner.

Bennett, too, was an influential contributor to the victory. Remarkably, he was the visitors' third choice fly-half for this particular match. Firstly John Bevan, and then David Richards, had withdrawn due to injuries, with the Llanelli player ultimately taking their place, for his 18th appearance in the Wales jersey. The occasion was also special in his case in that it was the first time that he had played for a victorious Wales team away at Twickenham. He kept his place in the team and by the end of that international season he had amassed 38 points, which was a record for any Welsh player in the Championship.

He did not appear among the scorers at Twickenham but, with England still in contention following three penalties by Hignell, he had a crucial role in the final Wales try when a curving run and a scintillating scissors with J.P.R. saw the full-back crash over the line once again. The Wales kickers also made their mark during the game, with Fenwick converting all three tries and Allan Martin kicking a penalty goal.

38

5 March 1977: Arms Park, Cardiff

14–9: Wales won by 2 tries and 2 penalty goals to 3 penalty goals

Wales: J.P.R. Williams (Bridgend); G. Davies (Cardiff), S.P. Fenwick (Bridgend), D. Burcher (Newport), J.J. Williams; +P. Bennett (Llanelli), G.O. Edwards (Cardiff); C. Williams (Aberavon), R.W. Windsor, G. Price (Pontypool), A.J. Martin (Aberavon), G. Wheel (Swansea), R.C. Burgess (Ebbw Vale), D.L. Quinnell (Llanelli), T.J. Cobner (Pontypool).

England: A.J. Hignell (Bristol); P.J. Squires (Harrogate), B.J. Corless (Moseley), C.P. Kent (Rosslyn Park), M.A.C. Slemen (Liverpool); M.J. Cooper (Moseley), M. Young (Gosforth); R.J. Cowling, P.J. Wheeler (Leicester), F.E. Cotton (Sale), W.B. Beaumont (Fylde), N.E. Horton (Moseley), M. Rafter (Bristol), +R. Uttley, P.J. Dixon (Gosforth).

England were playing to win their first Triple Crown since 1960 but, although leading by 9–7 at half-time, they were thwarted once again. Indeed that achievement belonged to Wales following their subsequent victory over Scotland. Yet despite having a greater points aggregate than France, the latter achieved the Grand Slam and took the Championship.

Regardless of the scintillating talents of the Welsh backs, the key to the home team's victory lay in the control established by their forwards, with new cap Clive Williams, deputising at loose head for the injured Charlie Faulkner, having a storming debut. The match confirmed his reputation as a formidable scrummager and his impressive performance led to his being selected to tour New Zealand with the British Lions in 1977. Ironically, on his return, he lost his place in the Aberavon team to John Richardson, who was also capped by Wales the following season. Williams joined Swansea and, having regained his place in the Wales team in 1980, toured South Africa with the British Lions later that year, playing in four Tests.

In the light of earlier games that season the 1977 match against England elicited a complete reversal of form for both teams, in that the visitors' pack had previously dominated their opponents while their Welsh counterparts had struggled against France and Ireland. (Ironically, too, in clinching the Triple Crown two weeks later at Murrayfield Wales were once again well beaten at forward.) Yet despite the home pack's superiority Hignell kicked England to a six-point lead before Wales opened their account with a typically unstoppable Gareth Edwards try from a five-yard scrum. Their only other score in the first half was a penalty goal by Fenwick, while Hignell converted his third successful kick.

With Gareth Edwards superbly orchestrating the Wales performance and Bennett excelling in attack and defence, the home team went ahead through another Fenwick penalty goal before sealing the victory with yet another magnificent J.P.R. try. Capitalising on excellent line-out ball from Martin, centre David Burcher created a gap for Williams to storm through and, with the England defence caught napping as they anticipated a pass to the lethal Gerald Davies outside him, the full-back dummied and charged over the line.

This was Phil Bennett's final appearance against England at Cardiff and despite the fact that their defence had often been tormented by the Llanelli fly-half, they remained, upon his retirement from international rugby the following season, the only Championship side not to have conceded a try by Phil Bennett. Nevertheless, they were doubtless glad, as were so many other opponents, to be rid of his devastating influence on games between the two countries.

In his 29-cap career he captained his country on eight occasions, during which time they were victorious in all but one of the games. He was also captain of the 1978 British Lions team on their tour to New Zealand. However more renowned than his inspirational leadership was his exhilarating talent as an exponent of attacking rugby, in addition to his excellent kicking skills. He was involved in many memorable scores both as a pernicious instigator and a devastating finisher.

In the words of one of his English contemporaries, David Duckham, 'he jinks and sidesteps with the speed and often numbing effect of a cobra's tongue'. According to the late Cliff Morgan, one of the greatest outside-halves ever, 'he made the game so exciting that you'd have paid an extra £10 on the gate if you'd have known he was going to be playing'. Carwyn James described his breathtaking contribution to that Barbarians try in 1973 as 'a rare and memorable moment when a player is playing at a level other than the conscious, the unique moment when the game almost assumes an art form'.

39

4 February 1978: Twickenham

9–6: Wales won by 3 penalty goals to 2 penalty goals

Wales: J.P.R. Williams (Bridgend); G. Davies (Cardiff), S. Fenwick (Bridgend), R. Gravell, J.J. Williams; +P. Bennett (Llanelli), G. Edwards (Cardiff); A. Faulkner, R.W. Windsor, G. Price (Pontypool), A. Martin (Aberavon), G. Wheel (Swansea), J. Squire (Newport), D.L. Quinnell (Llanelli), T. Cobner (Pontypool).

England: A.J. Hignell (Bristol); P.J. Squires (Harrogate), B.J. Corless (Moseley), P.W. Dodge (Leicester), M.A.C. Slemen (Liverpool); J.P. Horton (Bath), M. Young (Gosforth); B.G. Nelmes (Cardiff), P.J. Wheeler (Leicester), M.A. Burton (Gloucester), +W.B. Beaumont (Fylde), N.E. Horton (Toulouse), M. Rafter (Bristol), J.P. Scott, R.J. Mordell (Rosslyn Park).

This was again the first step on the trail towards another Triple Crown and Grand Slam for the visitors. Yet it was accomplished in a manner which was completely alien to the exciting style of play with which the Wales team had become associated in recent years. With this performance they showed that they could also win 'ugly' when the circumstances so demanded since it was an atrociously wet day with extremely heavy conditions underfoot.

It was also a day of milestones. It was the occasion of Gareth Edwards's 50th cap, a feat which was made all the more remarkable by the fact that they had been won consecutively. On the day it was recognised by his captain, Phil Bennett, in letting Gareth carry the ball as he led the team onto the field. In addition it was also his final appearance against England, which was also true of Phil Bennett. The nature of the encounter on the day meant that Wales failed to score a try against them for the first time since 1962, whereas England, during that period, failed to touch down against Wales on nine occasions.

In this particular match, in the driving rain, the home forwards were dominant, yet they were prevented from gaining any significant advantage by the magnificent play of Gareth Edwards. Ollie Burton, the England prop, is quoted by writer Huw Richards as follows:

> Gareth Edwards controlled the match like a conjuror thereby rendering all our muddy efforts in our little twilight world utterly useless and irrelevant. It didn't really matter who was on top, Gareth kicked the ball down behind us and broke our hearts. We could win two or three balls in succession, batter our way up field and be poised for an attack on the Welsh line then Gareth would send the ball rolling... into our twenty-five and we had to start again.

One relieving kick from the scrum-half, from the narrowest of angles, which landed 65 yards downfield and rolled into touch to put Wales in an attacking position, was deemed by many to be the highlight of the match.

England, through two penalty goals by Hignell, led by six points to three at half-time, while Bennett was the visitors' successful kicker. After the interval he added another to bring the scores level and then, with eight minutes remaining, R.J. Mordell, the home team's Number 8, who was making his international debut, was penalised for handling in the ruck. Bennett again kicked the resultant penalty goal to put Wales ahead for the first time and to give him a match success rate of three goals from four attempts, which, in the light of the heavy ball and the muddy conditions, was an excellent ratio. With just minutes to go Hignell had a chance to bring the scores level but, as in the case of four other attempts, the kick failed.

At the end of a game, which for him was significant and

memorable, Gareth Edwards had one more tussle to win as he sought a fitting trophy:

> ... by instinct, I raced around looking for the ball... I discovered the ball under three or four forwards, all scrapping for it. I managed to get a couple of fingers on a panel. Mike Rafter was hanging on for dear life but Charlie Faulkner was on top and Bobbie Windsor in there too. 'Aw. C'mon lads. Let me have it this time,' I said pathetically.
>
> 'Yes,' Bobbie chipped in. 'C'mon lets give it to Gareth.' As soon as Mike was given room to breathe he said 'Yes sure. It's yours Gareth.' I will not forget that either. Poor Mike had a harder time fighting for that ball with Faulkner and Windsor than he had in the whole match... On to the Hilton and a superb banquet. The Rugby Union made a great gesture. On their behalf I was presented with a beautiful Spode porcelain bowl. It was number fifty.

40

17 March 1979: Arms Park, Cardiff

27–3: Wales won by 5 tries, 2 conversions and 1 drop goal to 1 penalty goal

Wales: +J.P.R. Williams (Bridgend); E. Rees (Neath), D.S. Richards (Swansea), S.P. Fenwick (Bridgend), J.J. Williams (Llanelli); W.G. Davies, T.D. Holmes (Cardiff); S.J. Richardson (Aberavon), A.J. Phillips (Cardiff), G. Price (Pontypool), A.J. Martin (Aberavon), M.G. Roberts (London Welsh), J. Squire (Pontypool), D.L. Quinnell, P. Ringer (Llanelli).

Replacement: C.R. Griffiths (Llanelli) for J.P.R. Williams.

England: A.J. Hignell (Bristol); P.J. Squires (Harrogate), R.M. Cardus (Roundhay), P.W. Dodge (Leicester), M.A. Slemen (Liverpool); W.N. Bennett (London Welsh), P. Kingston (Gloucester); C.E. Smart (Newport), P.J. Wheeler (Leicester), G.S. Pearce (Northampton), +W.B. Beaumont (Fylde), N.E. Horton (Toulouse), M. Rafter (Bristol), J.P. Scott (Cardiff), A. Neary (Broughton Park).

This was the match that secured the Triple Crown for Wales for the fourth successive season. Although they also won the Championship for the second successive season, they had been denied the opportunity to achieve the Grand Slam when France defeated them by one point. For this particular game Wales fielded eight players who had not appeared in the previous season's match against England. This was as a result of the retirement from the international scene of stalwarts Gerald Davies, Edwards, Bennett and Cobner, injuries to Faulkner, Windsor and Wheel, while Ray Gravell had lost his place to David Richards.

After their debut for Wales in 1975 the 'Pontypool Front

Row' made nine consecutive appearances before an injury to Faulkner saw him miss the 1977 internationals. The partnership was then resumed for the next ten consecutive internationals, until this particular match, when Charlie withdrew with an injury to his knee while Bobby had been hospitalised with first- degree burns to his back from lime used to mark the pitch when playing for Pontypool the previous week.

The visitors, following their hard-earned victory against France, were the favourites to win, an outcome which had been confidently predicted by their skipper, Bill Beaumont, before the game. However, they suffered their heaviest defeat against Wales since losing 25–0 in 1905 and were completely outplayed. Despite the fact that their pack were well in control from the outset, the home team, with 20 minutes remaining, led by just 7–3 as a result of a try by Richards and a drop goal by Davies.

Then the floodgates opened, with Wales scoring 20 points in as many minutes. J.J. Williams crossed for his twelfth try for his country on this the occasion of his 30th consecutive cap. Thirty-three-year-old second-row Mike Roberts, the game's star player, following a line-out near the visitors' line, 'sprinted' over from all of 36 inches, the furthest, he claimed, he had ever run to score! He was winning his eighth cap, having made his international debut in 1971 against England! Paul Ringer crossed for another try before Elgan Rees, following excellent work by replacement full-back Clive Griffiths, who was winning his first and only cap, touched down for the last of five tries. Griffiths had come on for J.P.R. Williams who needed eight stitches in a nasty leg-wound. The Llanelli full-back made a notable contribution to the victory and was denied a debut try when his thrilling run from defence culminated in his being beaten to the touchdown by the speedy Rees. At the end of the season Griffiths joined St Helens Rugby League Club.

After failing with five penalty attempts, Steve Fenwick's single conversion (Allan Martin kicked the other) gave him a

Championship total of 38 points to equal the record previously set by Phil Bennett. The visitors' points came from a Neil Bennett penalty goal, which meant that for four consecutive seasons they had failed to score a try against Wales. Indeed, between 1976 and 1978 all England's points against them were the result of the eight penalties kicked by Alistair Hignell.

This particular match was the full-back's last international and he retired the following season at the age of 24 years to concentrate on his career as a first-class cricketer with Gloucester. He became a respected radio commentator on rugby matches for the BBC, a career which he pursued until 2008. In recognition of his services to broadcasting the Welsh Rugby Union presented him with a framed Welsh shirt on the occasion of his last broadcast from Cardiff. In 1999 he had been diagnosed with multiple sclerosis for which he has been an active campaigner ever since.

41

17 January 1981: *Arms Park, Cardiff*

21–19 : Wales won by 1 try, 1 conversion, 1 drop goal and 4 penalty goals to 1 try and 5 penalty goals

Wales: J.P.R. Williams (Bridgend); R. Ackerman (Newport), +S.P. Fenwick (Bridgend), D.S. Richards (Swansea), D.L. Nicholas (Llanelli); W.G. Davies (Cardiff), D.B. Williams (Swansea); I. Stephens (Bridgend), A.J. Phillips (Cardiff), G. Price (Pontypool), G. Wheel (Swansea), C. Davis (Newbridge), J. Squire (Pontypool), G. Williams (Bridgend), R. Lewis (Cardiff).

England: W.H. Hare (Leicester); J. Carleton (Orrell), C.R. Woodward, P.W. Dodge (Leicester), M.A.C. Slemen (Liverpool); J.P. Horton (Bath), S.J. Smith; F.E. Cotton (Sale), P.J. Wheeler (Leicester), P.J. Blakeway (Gloucester), +W.B. Beaumont (Fylde), M.J. Colclough (Angoulême), M. Rafter (Bristol), J.P. Scott (Cardiff), D.H. Cooke (Harlequins).

Replacement: A. Sheppard (Bristol) for Cotton.

It was an error-strewn game punctuated by much kicking, yet an event of notable milestones. J.P.R. Williams representing his country for the 54th time overtook Gareth Edwards's record as the most capped Welsh player. The match produced nine successful penalty goals, the highest number ever in the Championship, until Ireland's game against England two years later when Ollie Campbell and Dusty Hare kicked five penalties each. Indeed in 1981 there was a dearth of tries with the five countries between them only getting 25 touch downs (while the previous season their aggregate total was 40 tries). Wales was the biggest culprit in that they managed to cross their opponents' line on only two occasions in 1981.

Ten minutes into the game Steve Fenwick opened the scoring with a penalty goal, after England were guilty of obstruction at the back of a two-man line out in their 22. After 15 minutes, in the last of his 31 appearances for England, Fran Cotton was forced to leave the field with a pulled calf-muscle. Wales went further ahead when Gareth Davies produced a probing grubber kick to the right-hand corner. Wheeler, Hare and then Smith dithered in attempting to clear their lines, for the Welsh forwards to pounce and feed Clive Davis who charged over from two metres. Hare reduced the arrears for the visitors with his first penalty from 35 metres. Following a drive into the England 22 by the Wales forwards Fenwick added another penalty goal which was countered with another by Hare, who then touched down for a try. A scintillating handling movement on the Wales 22 by the visitors' three-quarters saw Dodge burst through from some 15 metres out, to give a half-time score of 12–10.

A ding-dong kicking battle ensued in the second half. Firstly Hare added another penalty goal to put his team ahead for the first time. Their lead didn't last long however, for Gareth Davies hit back with an excellent right-footed drop goal from some 35 metres out and to the left of the posts. Two more penalties from Hare, who on the day was responsible for all of England's points, and another from Fenwick, gave a scoreline of 18–19 with just a few minutes of the match remaining.

During injury time Wales had the put-in at a scrum outside their opponents' 22 as a result of which they were awarded a penalty. The incident is dramatically recalled in the autobiography *Winning* by the player responsible for incurring the penalty, Clive Woodward:

> I watched the Welsh scrum-half, Brynmor Williams, with one eye and my Welsh opposite number with the other. Williams fed the ball into the scrum and then moved around the back of the scrum to wait for it to emerge, poised to race off for one final attempt at the try line. Out of the corner of my eye, I saw him bend over for

the ball. He lunged towards his backs to start the attack. I raced off with a single focus of preventing them scoring. As if looking for me, Williams rounded the referee with his two hands held out, begging the call. The ref instantly blew his whistle and raised his hand to indicate an offside offence. I turned around in shock to see fourteen of my team-mates all standing beside the offside line, a couple of yards away. All behind, but me. All onside, but me. 'Shit!' I screamed in complete frustration and exasperation. I'd fallen for the oldest trick in the book.

Fenwick, of course, kicked the resultant penalty and although there was still time for an unsuccessful long-range attempt from the boot of Hare, England again were left waiting for their first victory in Cardiff since 1963.

42

17 March 1984: Twickenham

24–15: Wales won by 1 try, 1 conversion, 2 drop goals and 4 penalty goals to 5 penalty goals

Wales: H. Davies; M.H. Titley (Bridgend), R.A. Ackerman (London Welsh), B. Bowen (S.W. Police), A.M. Hadley (Cardiff); M. Dacey (Swansea), T.D. Holmes (Cardiff); I. Stephens (Bridgend), +M.J. Watkins (Newport), I. Eidman, R.L. Norster (Cardiff), S.J. Perkins (Pontypool), R.D. Moriarty (Swansea), E.T. Butler (Pontypool), D.F. Pickering (Llanelli).

England: W.H. Hare (Leicester); J. Carleton (Orrell), B. Barley (Wakefield), C.R. Woodward, R. Underwood; L. Cusworth, N.G. Youngs (Leicester); P.A.G. Rendall (Wasps), +P.J. Wheeler (Leicester), P.J. Blakeway (Gloucester), M.J. Colclough (Wasps), S. Bainbridge (Gosforth), A.F. Dun (Wasps), J.P. Scott (Cardiff), P.J. Winterbottom (Headingley).

With only six of the Wales team remaining from the side that played England at Cardiff the previous season all XV were able to celebrate being victorious at Twickenham in the Championship for the first time. It was the visitors' first win there for six years and their highest points total ever at that ground. The result meant that Wales had won both their Championship matches away from home but had lost the two played at Cardiff.

The game was a cut and thrust contest between, for the most part, two fairly evenly matched sides. The Wales backs, superbly marshalled by Malcolm Dacey, were the more enterprising. He was able to capitalise on an excellent service from Holmes whose probing runs also served as a constant threat. This was his first game for his country for eight months, having injured his knee when playing for the British Lions in the second Test against New Zealand the previous summer.

England, despite being under pressure in the line-outs, where Norster and Moriarty were dominant, enjoyed their fair share of possession, but indecision by their three-quarters in midfield frequently led to attacking efforts being thwarted. Indeed, for much of the time defences were on top which made for a game devoid of sparkle. A match aggregate of 39 points, which included just one try, perhaps bears testimony to that fact.

After Hare had put the home team ahead with a penalty goal after just three minutes, Wales hit back five minutes later when full-back Davies converted a penalty from 35 metres after Cusworth had been penalised for a high tackle on Bowen. The England full-back punished the visitors again with a penalty kick from 35 metres, but with six minutes of the half remaining, a try line was threatened for the first time. Titley kicked ahead out wide on the England 22-metre line, for Perkins to gather the loose ball and feed Pickering. The flanker charged over the line to touch down, only for the referee to disallow the score because it had been accomplished as the result of a double movement.

With the interval approaching, a penetrating blind-side break by Dacey just inside the Wales half, ably supported by Holmes, put England under pressure inside their 22. In trying to stifle the Wales three-quarters they conceded another penalty, which Davies converted to make the score 6–6 at the interval. Five minutes into the second half Hare again put his side ahead with an excellent penalty kick from his own ten-metre line, only to be countered once again when Winterbottom strayed off-side in front of his posts to give Davies an easy 20-metre kick to bring the scores level again.

Then four minutes later came the most exciting move of the match. Bowen, taking the ball from Dacey at inside centre, dummied to Ackerman and cut inside Cusworth. Running across-field from right to left Bowen linked with Hadley who stepped at pace inside the covering defence. He transferred to Butler who, on being checked five metres from the line, passed the ball back inside for the winger to cross under the posts. Davies kicked an easy conversion to put Wales ahead for the first time, by 15–9.

After 54 minutes a probing kick by Dacey saw an under-pressure England defence yield another penalty which was duly converted by Davies to give him a total of 39 points in the 1984 Championship, thus breaking the record, for a Wales player, of 38 points which had been shared until then by Phil Bennett and Steve Fenwick. Hare kicked another penalty goal to make the score 18–12, then with ten minutes remaining, Dacey kicked an excellent drop goal from 35 metres. Against the run of play England clawed their way back to 20–15 with another Hare penalty goal from 15 metres in front of the posts, but the Wales fly-half sealed the victory with another magnificent drop goal from a similar position to his first.

This was the outside-half's finest match for Wales. First capped the previous season against England, he demonstrated in this game, on the occasion of the tenth of his 15 caps, that he had matured into a shrewd and influential general of the Wales three-quarters. During his tenure in the Wales team he and Gareth Davies were the subject of much debate as to whom of the two was the more deserving of their country's Number 10 jersey. Before this particular match Dacey had been described by Peter Wheeler, the England captain, as the most improved player in the home countries and who was the hub of the dangerous Welsh backs. Taking advantage of the superb service given by Terry Holmes, Dacey, according to one press report, 'dominated the Twickenham stage... with a performance which bristled with authority and conviction'.

43

20 April 1985: Arms Park, Cardiff

24–15: Wales won by 2 tries, 2 conversions, 3 penalty goals and 1 dropped goal to 1 try, 1 conversion, 2 penalty goals and 1 dropped goal

Wales: P. Thorburn (Neath); P. Lewis (Llanelli), R.A. Ackerman (London Welsh), K. Hopkins (Swansea), A.M. Hadley (Cardiff); J. Davies (Neath), +T.D. Holmes (Cardiff); J. Whitefoot (Cardiff), W.J. James (Aberavon), S. Evans (Swansea), S.J. Perkins (Pontypool), R.L. Norster, G.J. Roberts (Cardiff), P. Davies, D.F. Pickering (Llanelli).

England. C.R. Martin (Bath), S.T. Smith (Wasps), K.G. Simms (Liverpool), +P.W. Dodge, R. Underwood (Leicester); C.R. Andrew (Nottingham), N.D. Melville (Wasps); A. Sheppard (Bristol), S.E. Brain (Coventry), G.S. Pearce (Northampton), J. Orwin (Gloucester), W.A. Dooley (Preston Grasshoppers), J.P. Hall (Bath), R. Hesford (Bristol), D.H. Cooke (Harlequins).

Both teams produced an exciting game on the day, yet the drama had commenced nine days previously, when the selectors announced the team for the match. Despite the fact that Gareth Davies was available for selection at outside-half, having played there in the three previous Championship fixtures, the position was filled by A.N. Other on the team sheet. Two days after the announcement Gareth and Malcolm Dacey would be in direct opposition in a club match between Swansea and Cardiff after which the selectors would seemingly choose between them for the Number 10 spot. To Gareth the implication of such action was that they no longer had confidence in him as the incumbent outside-half in the Wales team. His disappointment and anger were exacerbated by the fact that he heard of the selectors' plan via a third party and not directly from a WRU official.

In the light of such developments he informed the selectors that he no longer wished to be considered for the Wales team. In the game in question against Swansea he outplayed his rival, and the selectors chose Jonathan Davies to play his first game for Wales against England. He performed with distinction and made the position his own for the following three seasons, playing for his country in the next 15 Championship matches.

With Wales endeavouring to avoid a fifth successive home defeat England soon took the lead with a penalty by Andrew. This was soon cancelled out with a penalty from Thorburn after Cooke had strayed offside in a ruck. However, shortly afterwards, the Wales full-back was guilty of spilling a testing up-and-under by Andrew which saw the ball being moved along the visitors' three-quarter line, albeit rather slowly, until the introduction of full-back Martin put Simon Smith into space out on the right. The winger dashed over in the corner for Andrew to add the conversion to make the score 9–3 in England's favour.

After 23 minutes Wales reduced the arrears when Thorburn kicked another penalty goal. It resulted from a five-metre scrum which England had conceded following winger Lewis's tackle on Andrew behind the fly-half's own line. Similarly, a scorching movement involving Holmes, Pickering, Roberts and Perkins saw Wales cross the line, only for the referee to call another five-metre scrum at which the visitors were penalised yet again. Once more Thorburn was successful with the resultant penalty, as was Andrew again to make the score 9–12 after 36 minutes. However, just before half-time Wales levelled the score when a scruffy-looking drop-kick from Jonathan Davies scraped over the bar.

Terry Holmes, with several probing runs, was proving a constant thorn in England's side, and with Norster excelling in the line-out and Evans exerting his power in the close exchanges, Wales were gradually getting on top. Yet Andrew took England ahead for the fourth time when he dropped a goal from a line-out five metres from the home team's line. However, after 60 minutes an intended Garryowen from Jonathan Davies travelled much too far, with fortuitous consequences. Full back Martin completely misread the descent of the ball and fumbled it behind his own line, for the pursuing Davies to pounce and touch down. The try, which Thorburn converted, was the first by a Wales outside-half making his first appearance for his country since Ralph had scored a debut fly-half try against France in 1931.

Towards the end of the game Wales increased their lead with a sparkling move. Good driving work by the pack saw Jonathan Davies break through the visitors' defence only for his pass to fall behind Lewis. Hadley picked up the loose ball and fed Hopkins who transferred to Lewis. The winger passed to the supporting Pickering who, with a determined 15-metre foray, was held up just short of the line. However, the industrious Gareth Roberts was on hand to take the ball and crash over the line. Thorburn converted to make the final score 24–15.

This was Terry Holmes's final Championship appearance and his first as captain. He skippered Wales on one more occasion, against Fiji in November, before turning professional with Bradford Northern. He won 25 caps for his country and scored nine tries. Most of those were scored in his inimitable fashion whereby he would take on the opposition from within ten metres and blast his way to the line, making full use of his explosive power and his piston-like hand-off.

44

7 March 1987: Arms Park, Cardiff

19–12: Wales won by 1 try and 5 penalty goals to 4 penalty goals

Wales: M.A. Wyatt (Swansea); G. Webbe (Bridgend), K. Hopkins (Swansea), J. Devereux (South Glamorgan Institute/Bridgend), I. Evans (Llanelli); J. Davies (Neath), R.N. Jones (Swansea); J. Whitefoot (Cardiff), W.J. James (Aberavon), S. Evans (Neath), S. Sutton (S.W. Police), R.L. Norster (Cardiff), P. Moriarty (Swansea), P. Davies, +D.F. Pickering (Llanelli).

Replacement: R.G. Collins (S.W. Police) for P. Davies.

England: W.H.M. Rose (Harlequins); M.E. Harrison (Wakefield), K.G. Simms (Wasps), J.L.B. Salmon (Harlequins), R.E. Underwood (Leicester); C.R. Andrew (Wasps), +R.J. Hill; G.J. Chilcott, R.G. Dawe (Bath), G.S. Pearce (Northampton), W.A. Dooley, S. Bainbridge (Fylde), P.J. Winterbottom (Headingley), J.P. Hall (Bath), G.W. Rees (Nottingham).

'Ugly', 'brutal', 'dirty', 'violent' and other descriptions in that vein, summed up the general reaction of rugby pundits to this encounter. From the outset an intensely physical battle materialised, much of which did not involve the ball. At the second line-out the 6' 8" Dooley, in apparent retaliation for a punch directed at one of his colleagues, felled Phil Davies with a blow from behind. This resulted in multiple fractures to the Llanelli player's cheek, causing him to leave the field after seven minutes.

Dooley wasn't the only transgressor on the day and on the Monday following the match he was suspended by the Rugby Union, along with Dawe, Chilcott and Hill, 'for disciplinary reasons'. There was a feeling in the England camp however that the four offenders had been unjustly treated as Chilcot later reiterated:

> ... there is no doubt that the first five minutes would best be described as a brawl. Wade Dooley was one of those involved and darned nearly lost his job as a policeman over the incident... poor Richard [Hill] was banned even though he had no part in the fighting. Because he was the captain it was felt he should have had his lads under control. Quite how they thought he would prevent three 17-stone forwards throwing a punch single handed I am not sure. Another aspect of the lack of justice is that four England players were carpeted. The Welsh team were treated as heroes. Does anyone honestly believe that the scrapping was one sided?

Well, it seems that the Rugby Union did!

There were other casualties. Steve Sutton, also in that second line-out, suffered a fractured nose, caused by Norster's flailing arm, but stayed on the field until the end. Coincidentally, during a match between Cardiff and South Wales Police the previous season Sutton suffered an identical injury at the hands of the Cardiff player, when Norster threw a punch in retaliation which led to his receiving a ban which prevented him from representing his country in 1986.

The dour nature of the contest was reflected in the fact that 38 penalties were awarded during the match, with 23 of them for offences by England. Indeed of the 37 points scored 33 were the result of penalty goals, with Wyatt, deputising for the injured Thorburn, kicking five from nine attempts. England once again failed to score a try, as was the case in their earlier matches that season against Ireland and France. The four penalties kicked by Rose weren't his only rewarding experience. He collected coins from the pitch worth £3.50 which had been thrown at him by the crowd during the match. Having handed them to the referee for safekeeping he retrieved them after the game and spent them in the bar later that evening!

When England took an early lead from a Rose penalty goal

it was the only time in the match that they were ahead. Yet further successful kicks from him kept his team in the hunt throughout and at half-time they trailed by just 12–9. Wales extended their lead midway through the second half when Rees was penalised for obstruction and Wyatt once again secured the three points. This score was soon followed by the game's only try, engineered by Jonathan Davies. The fly-half, from a ruck on the opposition ten-metre line, having taken the ball on the open side switched to the narrow side and hoisted a huge kick towards the England line. Rose failed to gather cleanly, whereupon Underwood also fumbled the ball as the Wales forwards drove over him. Stuart Evans picked up five metres from the goal-line and, with three Englishmen on his back, the 17½-stone prop crashed over.

The visitors struck back with another Rose penalty goal, and in the closing stages crossed the Wales line on two occasions, through Dooley and Harrison. However, the former was held up by the powerful Wales forwards while the latter, under pressure from his opposite number, put a foot in touch as he grounded the ball. Wales held on deservedly for their only victory that season. They joined England at the foot of the table with just two points and avoided the Wooden Spoon only by virtue of a greater points' difference.

45

8 June 1987: Brisbane (World Cup)

16–3: Wales won by 3 tries and 2 conversions to 1 penalty goal

Wales: P.H. Thorburn (Neath); I. Evans (Llanelli), B. Bowen (S.W. Police), J.A. Devereux (South Glamorgan Institute/ Bridgend), A.M. Hadley (Cardiff); J. Davies (Neath), R.N. Jones (Swansea); A. Buchanan (Llanelli), A.J. Phillips (Cardiff), D. Young (Swansea), R.L. Norster (Cardiff), +R.D. Moriarty (Swansea), G. Roberts (Cardiff), P. Moriarty (Swansea), R.G. Collins (S.W. Police).

Replacement: H. Richards (Neath) for Norster.

England: J. Webb (Bristol); +M.E. Harrison (Wakefield), K.G. Simms (Wasps), J.L.B. Salmon (Harlequins), R. Underwood (Leicester); P. Williams (Orrell), R. Harding (Bristol); P. Rendall (Wasps), B.C. Moore (Nottingham), G.S. Pearce (Northampton), W.A. Dooley (Fylde), N. Redman (Bath), P.G. Winterbottom (Headingley), D. Richards (Leicester), G.W. Rees (Nottingham).

Replacement: G.J. Chilcott (Bath) for Rendall.

As an advertisement for the attractions of the inaugural World Cup this quarter-final game was a complete letdown. This miserable, dour encounter was described by Bob Templeman, the former Australian coach, as the worst game he had ever seen and that the All Blacks could play Wales and England at the same time and eat them for breakfast! England went into the match as favourites, despite having been well beaten by Australia at the group stage. Indeed, they had even booked their hotel accommodation for the semi-final stage in Brisbane to be held just under a week later! Wales, on the other hand, finished top of their pool, with victories against Ireland, Canada and Tonga.

However, an indifferent display against the Pacific islanders had not augured well for the quarter-final. England had been given the more comfortable ride up to that point in that they had played all their games at the Oval in Sydney, in pleasant weather, while Wales had been obliged to travel to three different locations in New Zealand. For the quarter-final they now had to journey the length of New Zealand from Invercargill, cross to Australia and then travel to Brisbane, before meeting England five days later.

Wales also had a serious selection problem with regard to the front row. Tight-head prop Stuart Evans had broken his ankle in the game against Tonga and John Rawlins, who had flown out to take his place, suffered a torn hamstring only minutes into his first training session after arriving. Jeff Whitefoot was also injured, so Dai Young, who was in Australia to play club rugby with Northern Suburbs, was pressed into service, thus winning the first of his 51 caps. In direct opposition initially to the experienced Paul Rendall, the 19-year-old Swansea prop gave a very good account of himself.

Critics were scathing in their analysis of a very poor performance by England. For Wales, Moriarty excelled in the line-out and was given excellent support by the back row. Norster, too, played his part, even though the value of his contribution was more psychological than physical. For the second-row was carrying an injured leg and should not really have played. However, manager Clive Rowlands considered that even a semi-fit Norster would have a considerable morale-boosting effect on his team, as well as being the cause of considerable trepidation amongst the opposition.

Such a shrewd tactical stroke proved to be even more valuable when it was learned that the England coach, Martin Green, perhaps mindful of the controversy that had surrounded Dooley following the previous game between the two countries, had decreed that the England second-row forward was not to jump in direct opposition to Norster in the line-outs. As a result the Wales jumper won an ample supply of ball during the first quarter, with Moriarty able to take control after Norster's injury had begun to impede his jumping ability.

Notwithstanding their disappointing performance overall, England were aggrieved that all three Welsh tries had been the result of errors on their part. While the injured Rendall was off the field, and before Chilcott could take his place, Gareth Roberts took advantage of an unsettled scrum to cross for Wales's first try. Then Robert Jones, making his 14th appearance in the red jersey, scored his first try for his country when he kicked through to beat Harding, the opposing scrum-half, to the touch down. The third try was scored by John Devereux when he ambled over the line following an interception. Paul Thorburn also contributed two conversions.

Despite the crucial contributions of some members of the pack to the victory, the outstanding player of the game was Robert Jones. His guiding influence and overall control in this particular match and throughout the tournament earned him the accolade of being the best European player of the 1987 World Cup. He went on to play 51 times for his country, only the second scrum-half to gain a half-century of caps. Despite having the misfortune, during that period, of playing behind a Welsh pack that was often inferior, he was acclaimed as a superb passer of the ball, even under pressure, which ensured that his fly-half invariably had impeccable service. His kicking, particularly from the base of the scrum and line-out, both in defence and attack, was of the highest quality and his reading of the game both astute and influential. These qualities were put to particular effect when Jones played a significant role on the successful British Lions tour to Australia in 1989, when the home side were defeated 2–1 in the Test series. The following season he endured the disappointment of being captain of the Wales team for five international matches which ended in defeat and included, for the fist time ever, a whitewash in the Five Nations Championship.

46

6 February 1988: Twickenham

11–3: Wales won by 2 tries and 1 drop goal to 1 penalty goal

Wales: A. Clement (Swansea); I. Evans (Llanelli), M.G. Ring (Pontypool), +B. Bowen (S.W. Police), A.M. Hadley (Cardiff); J. Davies (Llanelli), R.N. Jones (Swansea); S. Jones (Pontypool), K. Phillips (Neath), D. Young (Swansea), P. May (Llanelli), R.L. Norster (Cardiff), R. Phillips (Neath), P. Moriarty (Swansea), R.G. Collins (S.W. Police).

Replacement: I. Watkins (Ebbw Vale) for K. Phillips.

England: J.M. Webb (Bristol); +M.E. Harrison (Wakefield), W.D.C. Carling (Durham Univ./Harlequins), K.G. Simms (Wasps), R. Underwood; L. Cusworth (Leicester) N.D. Melville; P. Rendall (Wasps), B. Moore (Nottingham), J.A. Probyn (Wasps), J. Orwin (Bedford), W.A. Dooley (Fylde), M.G. Skinner (Harlequins), D. Richards (Leicester), P.J. Winterbottom (Headingley).

This fixture proved to be one of the most exciting between the two countries for many years. Indeed Wales had indicated beforehand how they intended to play the game. They selected four recognised fly-halves, Davies, Bowen, Clement, and Ring (who had been called up as a late replacement for the injured Devereux) even though such a decision courted controversy. For example, Anthony Clement was chosen at full-back in place of Paul Thorburn, who had previously kicked 140 points in 15 games. Up until then Clement had never played a full game for his country and had only ever played one game, with Swansea, at full-back at senior level. Yet Thorburn, despite his prowess as a kicker and defensive dependability, and unlike the Swansea youngster who replaced him for this game, was not known for his attacking flair. With that in mind the Wales coach, Tony Gray, was looking to field a team which could play expansive 15-man rugby.

Before the game critics pointed out that the Swansea player's inexperience in that position would make him vulnerable under pressure kicks from England, and indeed on the day that was a tactic frequently deployed by Cusworth, their outside-half. In fact it was used to excess in that they persevered with it at the expense of a possibly more rewarding style of play. Clement dealt admirably with the aerial bombardment and at times turned such a tactic to Wales's advantage.

The selected Wales outside-half, Jonathan Davies, had an outstanding match. Despite failing earlier with two attempted drop goals just before half-time, he almost put Wales ahead with a scintillating run. 'Mark Ring put me away on the halfway line. I dummied my way into a gap and went like hell for the line. The England full-back, Webb, bought the dummy but unknown to me made a great recovery – my legs were suddenly grabbed from under me.' It was certainly a try-saving tackle and, despite much enterprising play by both teams, the game was surprisingly scoreless at half-time.

The second half saw Welsh back-play at its best. Firstly, Clement, having fielded another up-and-under from Cusworth near his 22-metre line, went past two would-be tacklers and set up a ruck. The ball came to Bowen, then to Davies who passed to Ring, for the Cardiff centre to involve Clement once again. The full-back transferred to Hadley who cut inside and passed to Ring again before the two executed a telling scissors movement which saw Hadley move inside and then outside to touch down for a magnificent try.

Critics are of the opinion that the second Welsh try, which tore the English defence to shreds, was even better. With a curving run Jonathan Davies, near the halfway line, having switched the direction of play, linked with Ring. The centre ran strongly and, after throwing an audacious dummy to take out two English defenders, cut inside where his progress was halted. Collins picked up the loose ball and fed Norster who threw an overhead pass towards Bowen. He gathered and in turn passed inside to Hadley who drove over the line through the attempted tackles of Harrison and Cuthbert.

Then, after a Garryowen by Davies which put England under pressure in front of their own posts, the fly-half dropped a goal from the ensuing scrum. With his third attempt Jonathan Webb at last put his side on the scoreboard with a penalty goal to give a final score of 11–3. Wales, with exciting, attacking play emanating from an ample supply of good ball by their forwards, had once again denied England at Cardiff and proceeded on their victorious path to the Triple Crown, their first for nine years, and the Championship.

47

18 March 1989: Arms Park, Cardiff

12–9: Wales won by 1 try, 1 conversion and 2 penalty goals to 2 penalty goals and 1 dropped goal

Wales: +P.H. Thorburn (Neath); I. Evans (Llanelli), M.R. Hall (Cardiff), D. Evans (Cardiff), A. Emyr (Swansea); P. Turner (Newbridge), R.N. Jones (Swansea); M. Griffiths (Bridgend), I.J. Watkins (Ebbw Vale), L. Delaney, P. Davies (Llanelli), R.L. Norster (Cardiff), G. Jones (Llanelli), M.A. Jones (Neath), D. Bryant (Bridgend).

England: J.M. Webb (Bristol); R. Underwood (Leicester/RAF), +W.D.C. Carling (Harlequins), J.S.J. Halliday (Bath), C.J. Oti; C.R. Andrew (Wasps), C.D. Morris (Liverpool-St Helens); P. Rendall (Wasps), B. Moore (Nottingham), G.J. Chilcott (Bath), P.J. Ackford (Harlequins), W.A. Dooley (Preston Grasshoppers), M.C. Teague (Gloucester), D. Richards (Leicester), R.A. Robinson (Bath).

Replacement: G.W. Rees (Nottingham) for Teague.

Going into the match England were not only tipped to win but also to take the Championship as a result. They were undefeated in their previous three matches in the competition and had gained a convincing 11–0 victory against France two weeks previously. Wales, on the other hand, had lost their last three games and were facing the ignominy of suffering their first whitewash ever. Indeed they could claim just one victory, against Western Samoa, in their last eight matches.

There were two other factors which gave the visitors a definite advantage in advance of the kick-off. They had a settled team in that they had used just 16 players up to that point in the 1989 Championship, in contrast to the 23 who had appeared for Wales, including four new caps for this particular encounter. Secondly, their success had been built on dominant, driving displays by their forwards with scrum-half Dewi Morris in close support, for whom the weather conditions at Cardiff augured well. The pitch was heavy due to constant rain which had lashed Cardiff for hours before the start and which continued during the game.

However, England played as if the pre-match psychological ploys adopted by prominent figures in Welsh rugby had a disturbing effect upon them. For example, Brian Thomas was quoted as claiming that:

> The English are mentally inferior rugby-wise and as a race. Whenever I played against England I knew mentally that we were the better side. That can still happen – it's all a question of strength and will... [Morris] goes forward and makes the ball available but he can't pass. I can think of four Welsh scrum-halves who are better than him.

According to Barry John all Wales needed to do was to rattle Morris, for the whole team would then be rattled.

Indeed the home team were seemingly given a boost by the England coach himself. Geoff Cooke, mindful of English forwards' previous transgressions at Cardiff, had warned that the international career of any player who resorted to foul play would be terminated. It would have been obviously difficult to calculate to what extent the pre-match barbs had affected the visitors' performance, particularly the forwards, but their play was certainly inferior to that of the Welsh pack on the day.

Notwithstanding the antagonism which this particular fixture traditionally provoked, there were some players in the English ranks who had a direct connection with Wales. For example, Dewi Morris was a native of Crickhowell and a former pupil of Brecon Grammar School, but since he had played most of his rugby across the border he opted to play international rugby for his adopted country. He sang both anthems before the game but chose not to repeat the practice in future encounters! Flanker Mike Teague had turned out for Cardiff in previous seasons, as did Bill Carling, the father of the England captain, who played prop for the Blue and Blacks in 1966–67.

The resolute attitude of the home team was apparent straight from the kick-off when Mark Jones clattered recklessly into Teague, forcing him to leave the field. From the outset Robert Norster ruled the line-out, and the kicking of Robert Jones drove his team forward with relentless precision in the atrocious conditions. Consequently Wales, despite the visitors' carelessness in ignoring the unmarked Oti on two occasions when their opponents' line beckoned, had the better of the proceedings in the first half. Nevertheless, the score at the interval was 9–6 to England, the points coming from penalty kicks by Thorburn and Andrew and a scruffy drop goal by the fly-half which somehow scraped over the crossbar.

In the second half more telling kicks from Robert Jones were complemented by some damaging up-and-unders from his fly-half partner, Paul Turner, who, at the age of 30, was playing in his first Championship season and winning his third cap. He revelled in the task of exploiting the fallibility of the England defence under the high ball and one such kick led to the only try of the game, giving Wales the lead which they held until the end.

Although Underwood had caught Turner's kick safely, pressure from the home team's attackers forced him to throw a wild, inaccurate pass inside to Webb, which the full-back unsurprisingly failed to reach. In the ensuing melee Emyr kicked the ball on for Hall to slide over the line and win the race for the touch-down, which he appeared to dubiously execute with his fingertips. A try was awarded by the Australian referee, K.V.J. Fitzgerald, yet there were many that day who doubted the validity of that decision. Thorburn converted and Wales held on against an England team that became increasingly frustrated, with the result that the almost customary eruption occurred amongst the forwards leading to a brawl that lasted for half a minute.

Underwood blamed himself for the lapse that let in Wales for the try and was distraught in the changing room after the game. His misery was no doubt exacerbated upon reading the newspapers a few days later, for there he was given the name Rory Blunderwood. Scrum-half Morris, as a result of his disappointing performance, also suffered in the aftermath of the game in that he was not selected again for England for another three years.

Thorburn continued in antagonistic mode even after the final whistle. Leading up to the game certain members of the press had been very critical of recent performances by the Wales team. The *Sunday Times* correspondent Stephen Jones had even stated that he hoped that Wales would lose the match against England so that the shock of being whitewashed would force the WRU to take appropriate action to remedy the ills which were blighting the national team. Thorburn, obviously annoyed by such comments, made an obscene gesture towards the press box as he left the field and, at the start of his speech as captain at the official dinner after the match, he asked Stephen Jones to leave, as he considered him to be 'the scum of the earth'. Following his actions and despite being one of the leading full-backs in British rugby, and one of the most prodigious points scorers, he was omitted from the British Lions party to tour Australia some weeks later, although he was selected as a reserve.

48

6 February 1993: Arms Park, Cardiff

10–9: Wales won by 1 try (now worth 5 points), 1 conversion and 1 penalty goal to 2 penalty goals and 1 drop goal

Wales: M.A. Rayer (Cardiff); +I.C. Evans (Llanelli), M.R. Hall (Cardiff), I.S. Gibbs (Swansea), W.T. Proctor (Llanelli); N.R. Jenkins (Pontypridd), R.N. Jones (Swansea); R.L. Evans (Llanelli), N. Meek (Pontypool), H. Williams-Jones (S.W. Police), G.O. Llewellyn (Neath), A.H. Copsey, E. Lewis (Llanelli), S. Davies, R.E. Webster (Swansea).

England: J.M. Webb (Bath), I.G. Hunter (Northampton), +W.D.C. Carling (Harlequins), J.C. Guscott (Bath), R. Underwood (Leicester/RAF); C.R. Andrew (Wasps), C.D. Morris (Orrell); J. Leonard, B.C. Moore (Harlequins), J.A. Probyn (Wasps), M.C. Bayfield (Northampton), W.A. Dooley (Preston Grasshoppers), M.C. Teague (Moseley), B.B. Clarke (Bath), P.J. Winterbottom (Harlequins).

Replacement: P.R. de Glanville (Bath) for Hunter.

England had never been such strong favourites going into an encounter with Wales. On a magnificent run of form, having won their previous nine games, they were chasing a third consecutive Grand Slam. In their last three matches against Wales they had accumulated 34 points, 25 points and 24 points, whilst their opponents had amassed a grand total of 12 points. Indeed, during that three-year period, Welsh success at home in the Championship had been confined to just one victory and they had finished no higher that a shared bottom place in the table. In such a climate, defeat for the visitors at Cardiff in 1993 was inconceivable.

Indeed it appeared that the England team expected to win and with that in mind their attitude going into the game seemed coloured by complacency. Their comments in the press prior to the game suggested that the result was a foregone conclusion, with Brian Moore stating that it was impossible that England could lose the game. In Wales such apparent arrogance was tempered with a film produced by the BBC highlighting the fallibility of full-back Webb under the high ball and emphasising that England were 'beatable'.

There was no doubt that England were the better team on the day yet they were not allowed to flourish, despite an abundance of possession. Their three-quarter line was often harried into making mistakes due to intense pressure and resolute tackling by their opposite numbers, with Scott Gibbs proving to be the outstanding tackler on the field. The comparatively inexperienced Welsh front row confronted their more seasoned counterparts with dogged determination and Llewellyn performed admirably in the line-out. Although England were the heavier pack by just two pounds, their total of 248 caps to 56 for Wales meant that they had a massive advantage over their counterparts in terms of experience.

England took the lead after a few minutes when Webb kicked an excellent penalty goal from the Wales ten-metre line after the home team were punished for not releasing on the floor. Yet that was their only foray into the home team's territory for the next 20 minutes. During that period Wales were in control yet all they had to show for their dominance was an excellent penalty goal by Jenkins, after ten minutes, from two metres inside the England half, after Winterbottom went off-side at a ruck. With the Welsh pack successfully driving forward after a towering up-and-under from their fly-half, they crossed the line but were unable to secure a touch-down. However, all other efforts to score were well thwarted by stout defence from their opponents.

After 22 minutes a scintillating 40-metre run by Guscott, ably supported by Clarke, saw England gain a firm foothold in their opponents' half of the field, a position which they did not relinquish for the remainder of the first period. Morris, who was having an excellent game and who proved with his darting runs to be a constant thorn in the opposition's side, drove for the Wales line, after picking up from a five-metre scrum, and grounded the ball for what appeared to be a legitimate try. The referee, however, adjudged that in the act of scoring he had undertaken an additional movement after a tackle so the try was disallowed, which, on further analysis, appeared to be an erroneous decision.

Webb kicked another penalty goal, and storming runs by Teague and Carling served to underline the visitors' superiority. Further pressure saw a pass from Clarke fail to reach Guscott, only for the centre to pick up and from 30 metres out drop a left-footed goal to put England further ahead, by 9–3. However their lead did not last long, for Emyr Lewis, having taken a pass from Robert Jones five metres outside his 22, decided to kick ahead into the visitors' half, past the covering Underwood. The winger's casual turn and saunter to get to the ball allowed the undetected Ieuan Evans to shoot past him and kick the ball over the goal-line from under his nose. Webb, the last line of defence, as he saw the ball go by, tried despairingly to retrieve the situation but was no match for Evans whose scorching pace allowed him to reach the ball first and touch down. Jenkins converted to give Wales, against the run of play, a half-time lead of 10–9, despite Webb failing with a comparatively easy penalty attempt just before the interval.

England continued to exert constant pressure during the second half. Probing kicks to the corner placed the Wales line under pressure on more than one occasion. Another darting foray by Morris led to Bayfield losing the ball as he was endeavouring to touch down. Despite several promising runs by the visitors involving skilful handling movements between backs and forwards, the home team's tackling was of the highest order, which caused their opponents to become more desperate and careless as the game progressed. Morris, with a devastating burst from just inside the Wales half, almost reached the try line and Webb hit the post with a penalty attempt. Yet with Rayer in excellent defensive form and Jenkins continuously relieving English pressure with towering downfield Garryowen kicks, Wales, despite being on their heels throughout the second half, stood firm. The unexpected victory was not the most spectacular but certainly one of the most dogged.

49

11 April 1999: Wembley Stadium

32–31: Wales won by 2 tries, 2 conversions and 6 penalty goals to 3 tries, 2 conversions and 4 penalty goals

Wales: S.P. Howarth (Manchester-Sale); G. Thomas (Cardiff), M. Taylor, I.S. Gibbs (Swansea), D.R. James; N.R. Jenkins (Pontypridd), +R. Howley (Cardiff); P.J.D. Rogers (London Irish), G.R. Jenkins, B.R. Evans (Swansea), J.C. Quinnell (Richmond), C.P. Wyatt (Llanelli), C.L. Charvis (Swansea), L.S. Quinnell (Llanelli), B.D. Sinkinson (Neath).

Replacements: N.J. Walne (Richmond) for Thomas; A.L.P. Lewis (Cardiff) for Rogers; D. Young (Cardiff) for Evans.

England: M.B. Perry (Bath); D. Luger (Harlequins), J.P. Wilkinson (Newcastle), B-J. Mather, S.M. Hanley (Manchester-Sale); M.J. Catt (Bath), M.J.S. Dawson (Northampton); J. Leonard (Harlequins), R. Cockerill, D.J. Garforth, M. Johnson (Leicester), T.A.K. Rodber (Northampton), R.A. Hill (Saracens), +L.B.N. Dallaglio (Wasps), N.A. Back (Leicester).

Replacement: V.E. Ubogu (Bath) for Garforth.

Because the Millennium Stadium was under construction this 'home' game for Wales was played at Wembley. It was an occasion that will always be remembered for *the* Scott Gibbs try, two minutes into injury time, which enabled the 'home' team to snatch a last-gasp victory to deprive their opponents once again of a Grand Slam. England had consequently gone into the encounter as clear favourites and were on course to win their fifth successive Triple Crown and to set down the milestone of becoming the winners of the last ever Five Nations Championship, since Italy were to be admitted to the competition the following season. In the corresponding fixture at Twickenham the previous year they had defeated Wales by a record score of 60–26. The Welsh team had already lost to Scotland and Ireland in the 1999 Championship but surprisingly accomplished the redeeming achievement of dramatically defeating France in Paris, for the first time since 1975, just over a month prior to the Wembley encounter.

England started the game in champions 'mode' and within two minutes, following excellent handling, they went ahead when Luger was put into space by Perry to cross for a try under the posts, which Wilkinson converted. Indeed, during the first half they produced an entertaining fare of attacking adventurous rugby which culminated in two further tries. After 21 minutes, following slick handling by Dawson and Catt, 19-year-old winger Hanley, who had been hailed in English rugby circles as the new Jonah Lomu, went over for their second try. Their third try of the half was a gift from their opponents as Shane Howarth and Gareth Thomas ran into each other when trying to deal with a kick from Catt over the heads of his opposing three-quarter line, allowing Hill to touch down. Another telling contribution by the Bath fly-half saw him take England to within metres of adding a fourth try. Nevertheless, with Wilkinson kicking another conversion and two penalty goals, they finished the half with a healthy 25 points.

However, Wales were still in the hunt due to the faultless place-kicking of Neil Jenkins. On the occasions that his team managed to get some kind of foothold in the opponents' half the pressure exerted by his forwards in particular led to indiscipline and careless play by the opposing pack, with the result that Wales were awarded six penalties during the opening half, all of which were converted by their fly-half. Despite the exciting running of their opponents' three-quarters, Wales went into the break trailing by only seven points.

Their coach, Graham Henry, was a great admirer of Jenkins's distribution skills and his mastery of the flat pass which the fly-half utilised with such telling effect. However, it was his

Scott Gibbs dances his way towards the England line at Wembley
© Getty Images

effective use of the floating pass which led to Wales drawing level two minutes after the restart. His half-break was halted some ten metres from the England line. A powerful drive from the forwards saw the ball reach Jenkins again, for the outside-half to cleverly omit his centres as he passed directly to Howarth coming up on the right wing some 15 metres out. The full-back touched down and Jenkins himself converted to make it 25–25. Powerful work by the England forwards saw them make several incursions into their opponents' territory resulting in another two successful Wilkinson penalties and a six-point lead. However, by this time, Jenkins and Howarth were frequently repelling English advances with telling kicks yet with 15 minutes to go they almost increased their lead when another skilful handling movement saw Perry drop the ball within sight of the opposition goal-line.

With just minutes until full time they were awarded another penalty some 40 metres out and well within the kicking range of Wilkinson. However, skipper Dallaglio thought that it was best to go for touch and try to pin Wales in their own half. He deemed that, by so doing, they would be given no opportunity to battle their way downfield to within scoring distance, a decision which, it was almost unanimously agreed, cost his team their victory.

Although that kick to touch took play into the Wales 22, a dangerous tackle by Rodber on Charvis saw Jenkins take his team down to his opponents' 22-metre line with a magnificent penalty kick, with two minutes of injury time already played. A three-man line-out saw Chris Wyatt, who had excelled in that aspect throughout, soar above everybody and transfer the ball to Howley. He passed directly to Scott Quinnell who just managed to hold on to the ball. He in turn transferred to Scott Gibbs on the charge. The England defence might have been forgiven for thinking that the centre, once described by Jeremy Guscott as the world's fastest prop, would try to reach the goal-line via his customary practice of flattening anyone who stood in his way. In this instance, however, he displayed talents more akin to a dancer as he waltzed his way past Dawson, Rodber, Beck, Perry and Hanley, leaving them clutching thin air, to score a remarkable try, which has been voted in various opinion polls over the years as the best Welsh try ever.

With the score at 32–31 to England, Neil Jenkins still had to kick the conversion to ensure victory. Indeed, when Gibbs crossed the line Jenkins had been shouting at him to touch down nearer the posts to make the conversion a little easier, but in the deafening cauldron of sound that was Wembley at that moment his plea went unheard. Gibbs ran back, handed him the ball and said, 'Just f****** kick it'!

By his own admission Jenkins never got nervous when taking kicks, regardless of how crucial they might be. Even at King's Park, Durban, when playing for the Lions against South Africa, his kicking drill remained unchanged. He would take deep breaths and imagine he was back at Cae Fardre, a field near his home where he spent hours on end taking practice kicks as a young lad, thus blotting out all noise and removing all pressure. Therefore, while there were countless supporters' hearts in countless supporters' mouths before the Wembley conversion, which to them was by no means a formality, Jenkins, as usual, and with a minimum of fuss, from 35 metres out and 15 metres to the right of the posts, did the business to secure victory.

However, according to Graham Henry, 'England were the better side. We didn't play very well, giving away so many turnovers and missing tackles on the fringes. But we hung on in there!' There were many devastated Englishmen on the day, none more so than the many traders lined up outside the stadium, who, at the final whistle, had to pack away the England Grand Slam T-shirts that they had hoped to sell in their hundreds!

50

5 February 2005: Millennium Stadium

11–9: Wales won by 1 try and 2 penalty goals to 3 penalty goals

Wales: +G. Thomas (Toulouse); H. Luscombe (Dragons), T.G.L. Shanklin (Blues), G.L. Henson, S.M. Williams (Ospreys); S.M. Jones (Clermont Auvergne), D.J. Peel (Scarlets); G. Jenkins (Blues), D.M. Davies (Gloucester), A.R. Jones (Ospreys), B.J. Cockbain (Ospreys), R.A. Sidoli (Blues), D. Jones (Scarlets), M.E. Williams (Blues), M.J. Owen (Dragons).

Replacements: K.A. Morgan (Dragons) for Luscombe; G.J. Cooper (Dragons) for Peel; J.V. Yapp (Blues) for A. Jones; J.J. Thomas (Ospreys) for Cockbain; R.P. Jones (Ospreys) for D. Jones.

England: +J. T. Robinson; M.J. Cueto (Sale), M.J. Tait, J.D. Noon (Newcastle), O.J. Lewsey (Wasps); C.C. Hodgson (Sale), M.J.S. Dawson (Wasps); G.C. Rowntree (Leicester), S. Thomson (Northampton), J. White (Leicester), D.J. Grewcock (Bath), B.J. Kay (Leicester), C.M. Jones (Sale), J.P.R. Worsley (Wasps), A. Hazell (Gloucester).

Replacements: O.J. Barkley (Bath) for Tait; H.A. Ellis (Leicester) for Dawson; P.J. Vickery (Gloucester) for Rowntree; Rowntree for White; S.W. Borthwick (Bath) for Grewcock; J. Forrester (Gloucester) for Worsley (temp).

Just as Scott Gibbs was the national hero as a result of his match-winning achievement against England at Wembley in 1999 that mantle was transferred to another centre, Gavin Henson, following this particular game. With just four minutes of the game remaining, and with Wales trailing by 9–8, he kicked a magnificent 45-metre penalty goal five metres in from the right-hand touchline, to secure their first victory against England in Cardiff since 1993, en route to a subsequent Grand Slam. While Wales supporters were filled with trepidation as Henson took the kick, he later admitted that he knew all the while that he was going to score. Having been voted the IRB Young Player of the Year in 2001, he was making his 12th appearance for Wales, albeit his first in the Six Nations Championship.

England started the game badly and surprisingly lost the first three line-outs on their own throw. On the third occasion, after ten minutes, Wales spun the ball to the right and when that move was halted they then moved it left, which resulted in Shane Williams skipping over in the corner for a try, following a deft transfer by Henson to Michael Owen who lofted a well-judged pass to his winger. Hodgson had kicked a penalty goal for the visitors after a storming run by Grewcock, only for Stephen Jones, after 23 minutes, to take Wales further ahead also with a penalty goal. The home team was having the better of the encounter, which was exciting yet lacking in quality play, but failed to take advantage of its domination despite several promising moves, particularly down the left wing. However a towering kick from Henson saw Gareth Thomas catch Lewsey in possession. The resultant scrum led to a ruck at which Grewcock stepped forward and onto the head of Dwayne Peel. An aggrieved Thomas rushed over and pushed the second-row forcefully which resulted in both players being sent to the sin bin, with Henson moving temporarily to full-back in place of his skipper.

After eight minutes of the second half Hodgson added a second penalty goal for the visitors during a period when their pack was in the ascendancy. Replacement Barkley, on in place of Mathew Tait who had been given a torrid time at the hands of Henson, also began to drive Wales back with telling kicks. Tait, who was celebrating his 19th birthday the following day, was the youngest debutant to play for England since Jonny Wilkinson in 1998. Along with Cueto and White, he had been

Gavin Henson seals victory with a magnificent penalty goal
© Getty Images

subjected to a number of crunching tackles by Henson, which had a marked psychological effect on the Wales performance, particularly early on.

With ten minutes to go the visitors took the lead for the first time when Hodgson kicked another penalty goal, and despite subjecting their opponents to intense pressure, Wales were unable to capitalise. However, four minutes from the final whistle the home team were awarded the penalty that gave Gavin Henson instant fame and a victory by 11–9 to Wales. A clever kick by Cooper had put Robinson in all kinds of trouble which led to Lewsey transgressing by diving over the top in the ensuing ruck.

Andy Robinson, the visitors' coach, conceded that his team, on the night, having been turned over too often and having incurred too many penalties, had not deserved to come out on top. The winning score was the lowest since the 1993 victory against England, but bearing in mind that Wales in their previous six games against them had conceded 46, 44, 50, 26, 43 and 31 points respectively, this result was indeed to be welcomed. As a spectacle, however, the match was succinctly summed up by Simon Thomas in the *Western Mail*: 'It was the day when Wales won ugly thanks to their pretty boy.'

51

17 March 2007: Millennium Stadium

27–18: Wales won by 2 tries, 1 conversion, 4 penalty goals and 1 drop goal to 2 tries, 1 conversion, 1 penalty goal and 1 drop goal

Wales: K.A. Morgan (Dragons); M.A. Jones (Scarlets), T.G.L. Shanklin (Blues), +G. Thomas (Toulouse), S.M. Williams; J.W. Hook (Ospreys), D.J. Peel (Scarlets); G. Jenkins (Blues), M. Rees (Scarlets), C. Horsman (Worcester), I. Gough, A.W. Jones (Ospreys), A.J. Popham (Scarlets), M.E. Williams (Blues), R.P. Jones (Ospreys).

Replacements: M. Phillips (Ospreys) for Peel; D. Jones (Ospreys) for Jenkins; T.R. Thomas (Blues) for Rees; A. Jones (Ospreys) for Horsman; J. Thomas (Ospreys) for Popham.

England: M.J. Cueto (Sale); D. Strettle (Harlequins), M.J. Tait (Newcastle), +M.J. Catt (London Irish), J.T. Robinson (Sale); T.G.A.L. Flood (Newcastle), H. Ellis (Leicester); T. Payne (Wasps), G. Chuter, J. White, M. Corry (Leicester), T. Palmer, J. Haskell, J. Worsley, T. Rees (Wasps).

Replacements: S. Geraghty (London Irish) for Catt; S. Perry (Bristol) for Ellis; S. Turner (Sale) for Payne; L. Mears (Bath) for Chuter; L. Deacon (Leicester) for Palmer; M. Lund (Sale) for Worsley.

Once again the odds were stacked firmly in England's favour before the game. On this the last day of the Six Nations competition, four teams had hopes of becoming champions, namely Italy, Ireland, France and England. However, by the time this particular game kicked off, England knew that to gain that honour and overtake France, who like the other teams had played earlier in the day, they had to win this encounter in Cardiff by a margin of 57 points. Wales, on the other hand, had lost their previous five matches to New Zealand, Ireland, Scotland, France and Italy, conceding 140 points in the process and in this encounter with England were endeavouring to avoid the Wooden Spoon.

The architect of the Welsh victory, James Hook, was making his first appearance in the Six Nations Championship at outside-half by default, as it were. For Stephen Jones had initially been selected in that position but had to withdraw through injury. Hook had an outstanding game, scoring 22 points, achieved by every possible scoring method. He had an auspicious start, for after just two minutes he charged down an attempted clearing kick by Flood close to the England line, gathered, and touched down for a try. He added a penalty goal after 11 minutes when the visitors had been penalised for incorrect binding at a scrum some 35 metres out, and four minutes later Wales went further ahead when a pass from Thomas sent Gethin Jenkins on a bulldozing 20-metre run. He was stopped just short of the try line but from the ensuing ruck Horsman burrowed over for his only international try to give Wales a comfortable 15–0 lead.

Up until this point the visitors had been guilty of frequently yielding possession and were for the most part penned in their own half. Their captain, Mike Catt, admitted after the match that they had been lucky not to have conceded more tries during this period as a fired-up Wales had dominated play. However, an excellent break by Catt on his own ten-metre line gave his team some redemption as he raced through midfield unimpeded. On his opponents' 22-metre line he chipped ahead, for the bounce to evade himself and the covering Jones, Hook and Thomas, only for the pursuing Ellis to ground the ball for a try. Flood converted, and after 34 minutes added a drop goal following a period of consistent English pressure.

Wales increased their lead with a Hook penalty goal but the visitors kept in contention with another magnificent try. Ellis sliced through the home defence from a ruck inside his own half, and when challenged on the Wales 22-metre line he fed Robinson on his left with an excellent long pass. The winger raced for the corner and at the last instant cleverly stepped inside the covering Hook and Jones to crash over the line, making the score 18–15.

Despite a penalty goal by Flood after five minutes of the second half, which brought the sides level, England failed to gain any momentum. Wales gradually took control, yet were guilty of wasting scoring opportunities. However, a period of continuous pressure from the home team saw Hook kick another penalty goal and a drop goal and then with six minutes remaining he completed his tally of 22 points with a magnificent penalty goal from near the halfway line to seal the victory. As a result, France were declared the Six Nations Champions and Scotland obtained the Wooden Spoon.

52

2 February 2008: Twickenham

26–19: Wales won by 2 tries, 2 conversions and 4 penalty goals to 1 try, 1 conversion, 3 penalty goals and 1 drop goal

Wales: L. Byrne (Ospreys); M. Jones (Scarlets), S. Parker, G. Henson, S. Williams; J. Hook, M. Phillips; A.R. Jones, H. Bennett, D. Jones, A.W. Jones, I. Gough, J. Thomas (Ospreys), M. Williams (Blues), +R. Jones (Ospreys).

Replacements: A. Popham (Scarlets) for J. Thomas; T. Shanklin (Blues) for Parker; G. Jenkins (Blues) for A.R. Jones; M. Rees (Scarlets) for Bennett; I. Evans (Ospreys) for A.W. Jones.

England: I. Balshaw (Gloucester); P. Sackey (Wasps), M. Tindall (Gloucester), T. Flood (Newcastle), D. Strettle (Harlequins); J. Wilkinson (Newcastle), A. Gomarsall (Harlequins); A. Sheridan (Sale), M. Regan (Bristol), +P. Vickery, S. Shaw (Wasps), S. Borthwick (Bath), J. Haskell (Wasps), L. Narraway (Gloucester), L. Moody (Leicester).

Replacements: L. Vainikolo (Gloucester) for Strettle; T. Rees (Wasps) for Moody; B. Kay (Leicester) for Rees; L. Mears (Bath) for Regan; D. Cipriani (Wasps) for Tindall; M. Stevens (Bath) for Vickery.

This was another game that Wales were expected to lose. Indeed they hadn't won at Twickenham since 1988 and their opponents hadn't lost an opening Six Nations fixture at home since 1983. To add fuel to the fires of pessimism, on their previous visit to Twickenham Wales had yielded 62 points. In addition, for this first game under the direction of new coach Warren Gatland, the team appeared to some critics to have been cobbled together on the basis of convenience rather than merit, since it contained 13 players from the Ospreys club, with yet another taking the field as a replacement.

The first half, which was dominated by the home team certainly seemed to confirm the likelihood of a Wales defeat. England went ahead after just one minute when Martyn Williams was penalised and Wilkinson put over the resultant kick from 40 metres. Hook kicked a penalty goal to draw the teams level but Wales were struggling to keep their opponents at bay. They frequently conceded possession and at times their defence was found wanting, which was particularly illustrated when Strettle produced a brilliant run, courtesy of several ineffectual tackles. However, his decision to kick near the line as opposed to passing to the unmarked Sackey let Wales off the hook.

Wilkinson put his team further ahead with another penalty and a drop goal and was instrumental in the move which led to the first try of the match. The fly-half, spotting that Mark Jones was in a 'one against one' situation with burly replacement Vainikolo, put in a pinpoint cross-field kick for the Gloucester winger to out-jump his opponent and off-load to Flood, who crossed near the posts, giving Wilkinson an easy conversion.

Following a line-out obstruction by Sheridan against Popham, Hook kicked a second penalty goal. Surprisingly his team was still within ten points of the home team, despite appearing at times to be in danger of being overrun by a rampant England side. With half-time approaching, further pressure by the home team in the Wales 22 almost brought another try when Sackey crashed over the goal-line only for Bennett, assisted by Hook, to remarkably succeed in getting his arm under the ball before the winger could touch it down. With Welsh concerns revolving around possible measures of damage limitation for the second half a revival seemed but an extremely distant possibility.

However, that is precisely what occurred, but not before Wilkinson had put his team further ahead with another penalty following a line-out offence by the visitors. Wales held firm and began to play with greater cohesion, yet going into the final quarter they still trailed by the seemingly insurmountable total of 19–6. An offence by Haskell led to Hook converting his third penalty goal to reduce the deficit, and a quickly taken kick by Shane Williams led to Henson decisively sidestepping past Wilkinson and the England defence, which was now in rapid retreat. This gave Wales a platform from which further pressure saw Balshaw penalised for not releasing in his 22, leaving Hook with a fairly easy kick to take the score to 19–12 after 62 minutes.

With shades of panic creeping into England's play, a dreadfully ballooned pass in midfield from Wilkinson over the head of his inside centre, Flood, which landed some metres behind Cipriani, put his side in considerable difficulty and paved the way for a crucial Wales try. A series of drives saw the ball in due course being moved left to Hook, who, having danced his way through three potential tackles, cleverly put the supporting Byrne over in the corner. A magnificent touchline conversion from the fly-half meant that the teams were now level on 19 points each.

Three minutes later the home team created more problems for itself. Balshaw took too much time over an attempted clearance in midfield just inside his own half, with the result that Phillips was able to charge down his kick. Gethin Jenkins skilfully gathered the loose ball at pace and fed Martyn Williams who transferred to Phillips, to see the scrum-half crash through Balshaw's last-ditch tackle to touch down and put Wales ahead for the first time in the match, with ten minutes remaining. Another magnificent touchline conversion by Hook meant that the outside-half had excelled once again, having converted six kicks from six attempts.

For the remainder of the match, with their pack controlling possession in the England half, Wales held their opponents in check, apart from one 20-metre burst by Haskell to take his team up to the halfway line in the final minute. Therefore, not for the first time, England, when the final whistle blew, found it hard to believe that they had let a convincing lead slip so dramatically and that the form which they had displayed so industriously in the first half had disastrously dissipated during the latter part of the game. In their defence they were forced during the match to make a number of substitutions in key positions due to injury. However Welsh supporters, when attempting to explain the reversal of fortunes which befell both teams, prefer to believe that the crucial factor was the quality of the team-talk in the visitors' changing room during half-time!

53

14 February 2009: Millennium Stadium

23–15: Wales won by 1 try and 6 penalty goals to 2 tries, 1 conversion and 1 drop goal

Wales: L. Byrne (Ospreys); L. Halfpenny, T. Shanklin, J. Roberts (Blues), M. Jones; S. Jones (Scarlets), M. Phillips (Ospreys); G. Jenkins (Blues), M. Rees (Scarlets), A. Jones, I. Gough, A.W. Jones, +R. Jones (Ospreys), M. Williams, A. Powell (Blues).

Replacements: H. Bennett (Ospreys) for Rees; D. Jones (Scarlets) for Powell; D. Peel (Sale) for Phillips.

England: D. Armitage (London Irish); P. Sackey (Wasps), M. Tindall (Gloucester), R. Flutey (Wasps), M. Cueto (Sale); A. Goode (Brive), H. Ellis (Leicester); A. Sheridan (Sale), L. Mears (Bath), P. Vickery (Wasps), +S. Borthwick (Saracens), N. Kennedy (London Irish), J. Haskell, J. Worsley (Wasps), N. Easter (Harlequins).

Replacements: D. Hartley (Northampton) for Mears; J. White (Leicester) for Vickery; T. Croft (Leicester) for Kennedy; L. Narraway (Gloucester) for Haskell; T. Flood (Leicester) for Goode; M. Tait (Sale) for Sackey.

The two teams had experienced differing fortunes in recent games. Wales had beaten Australia before Christmas, and Scotland at Murrayfield in their opening game in the Championship. England, on the other hand, had experienced a mauling in the autumn internationals, when they conceded over 100 points in their three matches. While they recovered to beat Italy at Twickenham to open their Six Nations campaign, it had been a generally unconvincing performance.

Wales started purposefully as they went through the phases and engaged in several promising moves. Yielding to pressure by the home team, Vickery went off-side at a ruck after four minutes which gave Stephen Jones an easy penalty kick to open the scoring. His side were also aided by indiscriminate kicking from England which allowed Wales to profit from punishing counterattacks, with Byrne, Roberts and Phillips making valuable contributions. The visitors continued to offend which, after a stern warning from referee Kaplan, led to Tindall, on 15 minutes, being sent to the sin bin after playing the ball on the floor. Stephen Jones kicked the resultant penalty goal to put Wales 6–0 ahead. Vickery was the next player to be penalised for dropping the scrum when not binding properly, which resulted in Halfpenny adding three points to the Wales total with a kick from 40 metres.

Then suddenly, after 24 minutes, England burst into life. A jinking run from Flutey saw the forwards feed Goode who kicked ahead. In a 10 metre race between the wingers, Strettle got to the ball before Mark Jones to dive over for a try. Two minutes later Goode reduced the arrears further with a drop goal from a narrow angle. Incredibly, at that stage, with Wales dominating the game territorially and earning a number of penalties due to their opponents' indiscretions which had reduced them to 14 men, the home team were ahead by just one point.

The visitors had nevertheless done their homework to stifle what they had perceived prior to the match to be the most potent Welsh attacking ploy, namely surging runs at pace by Jamie Roberts. For, to counter this tactic, they had assigned flanker Joe Worsley to shadow the centre wherever he went. Consequently, whenever Roberts got the ball, the Englishman lay in waiting and invariably brought him down before he could do any damage. In set play, to accommodate Worsley in the back line, spectators witnessed the unusual sight of his outside-half, Goode, taking his place in the pack.

However, immediately after the interval Roberts did get away, with Halfpenny in support, forcing Goode to produce an important tackle. Unfortunately for England he received a yellow card (his country's eighth in three games) for not rolling away quickly enough, and Stephen Jones put his team further ahead with another penalty goal. Wales immediately benefited from their numerical advantage to score again following a sweeping movement. A strong tackle by Shanklin on Strettle saw the ball being released and transferred, 'poetically' in the words of *The Guardian*, along the line to Byrne, who skilfully drew Cueto to create an overlap for Halfpenny who raced away for a try. In Goode's absence the visitors continued to struggle and were fortunate not to yield more points.

Another Stephen Jones penalty goal appeared to put Wales out of sight at 20–8, but three minutes later England were back in contention as a result of another excellent try. Flutey broke through the hosts' defence and fed the supporting Vickery for Armitage to continue the move with a deceptive dummy and a weaving run which saw him touch down under the posts. By this time Flood had taken the field as a replacement for Goode and seemed to inspire his backs to greater efforts. Sackey came close to scoring another try, having reached a shrewd kick from Ellis before any of his opponents, but just failed to take the ball over the goal-line. However, the England fight-back was scotched with eight minutes remaining when further indiscipline allowed Jones to kick his fifth penalty goal and Wales to hold on. With this particular result they had now drawn level with England with regard to the number of victories each had achieved over the other, namely 53.

54

13 August 2011: Millennium Stadium

19–9: Wales won by 1 try, 1 conversion and 4 penalty goals to 3 penalty goals

Wales: J. Hook (Ospreys); G. North (Scarlets), J. Roberts (Blues), G. Henson (free agent), S. Williams (Ospreys); R. Priestland (Scarlets), M. Phillips (Bayonne); P. James (Ospreys), L. Burns (Dragons), C. Mitchell (Exeter), L. Charteris (Dragons), A.W. Jones (Ospreys), D. Lydiate (Dragons), +S. Warburton (Blues), T. Faletau (Dragons).

Replacements: Scott Williams (Scarlets) for Henson; A. Brew (Dragons) for Priestland; H. Bennett (Ospreys) for Burns; J. Turnbull (Scarlets) for A.W. Jones; R. Bevington (Ospreys) for P. James; P. James for Mitchell.

England: B. Foden (Northampton); M. Banahan (Bath), +M. Tindall (Gloucester), S. Hape (London Irish), M. Cueto (Sale); T. Flood (Leicester), R. Wigglesworth (Saracens); A. Corbisiero (London Irish), S. Thompson (Wasps), D. Cole (Leicester), L. Deacon (Leicester), C. Lawes, T. Wood (Northampton), H. Fourie (Sale), N. Easter (Harlequins).

Replacements: D. Care (Harlequins) for Wigglesworth; J. Haskell (Ricoh Black Rams) for Fourie; M. Stevens (Saracens) for Corbisiero; L. Mears (Bath) for Thompson; D. Armitage (London Irish) for Tindall; C. Hodgson (Saracens) for Flood; T. Palmer (Stade Français) for Deacon.

This second World Cup warm-up game against England (who had narrowly won the first by 23–19 at Twickenham the previous week) was another between the two countries which, in the light of the visitors' territorial superiority and abundance of possession, should have resulted in a comfortable victory for them. In an exciting yet error-riddled match, the overall superiority of their pack, who excelled in the tight and in their driving aggressive play at close quarters, was negated by the ineptitude of the team in open play. There was no creative input in midfield and, although they made ample progress territorially, their efforts in this respect frequently came to nothing and for the first time in 14 matches England failed to score a try. Indeed, they failed to gain a single point from a dozen incursions into the Wales 22. The home team, on the other hand, scored ten points from only four such visits to their opponents' 22. The visitors would also rue the fact that on five occasions they declined to attempt kickable penalty goals but chose instead to go for touch in the hope of capitalising from the ensuing line-outs. In addition, the tackle count for the match showed that the defensive capabilities of the home team had no mean bearing on England's lack of penetration, for they were required to complete 134 tackles compared to 72 by the visitors.

Some post-match comments provided a telling summary of England's deficiencies in attack. Their coach, Martin Johnson, said after the game, 'I've never seen a game like it – to dominate like that and not have the points... we had a real stranglehold on the game in terms of possession and let it slip... It feels like we could still be playing now and we wouldn't be scoring a try.' Paul Rees wrote in *The Guardian* of 'England's poverty of ideas and cumbersome, fumbling attacks which came to grief as much as a result of their own ineptitude as the selfless defiance of the home defence.' Perhaps the most succinct comment came from BBC Sport's on-line match-report which described the visitors' as having 'all the cutting edge of a flaccid balloon' and that the team gave the appearance of 'playing through treacle'!

Referee Alain Roland awarded 30 penalties during the match, which for the most part were the result of players' indiscipline. Indeed, at Twickenham the previous week, England had conceded just four penalties, whereas they had incurred that number after just four minutes in this particular encounter. Wales were just as guilty, in that all of the visitors' points came from penalty goals by Flood which had been awarded for offences arising from restarts.

There were some promising England moves early on. Henson, who was having a particularly effective game, succeeded in halting a threatening run by Hape. However, in so doing, he hurt his wrist which led to his having to leave the field later during the half with an injury which ultimately prevented him from taking part in the World Cup. The visitors almost scored after 13 minutes when a charging Banahan, who stood at 6' 7" and weighed 17 stone 9lbs, was remarkably prevented from grounding the ball over the line at the last second by the 5' 7" and 12 stone 8lbs Shane Williams, with James Hook on hand to snatch the ball from the England winger's grasp.

The teams were level at half-time, courtesy of two penalty goals apiece from Priestland and Flood. The latter gave his side the lead a minute after the restart, with another penalty goal following an offence by Jamie Roberts which saw the centre sin-binned for ten minutes. With just a quarter of the game remaining, Wales scored the only try of the game, for by this time they had gradually begun to assert themselves as their opponents seemingly appeared to tire. A series of attacking ploys took them to within metres of the England line, from where Hook, now playing at outside-half in place of the injured Priestland, somehow jinked past Cole, Haskell and Care, to touch down near the posts. His conversion followed, along with another penalty goal ten minutes later to make the score 16–9 in Wales's favour.

Despite Phillips being sent to the sin bin for being off-side at a ruck after 71 minutes, Wales stood firm and even increased their lead when Hook kicked a magnificent penalty goal from near the halfway line after Cueto had been penalised for not releasing. Compounding the visitors' dismay at being unable to convert their early dominance into points was the fact that for 20 minutes during the second half they had failed to take advantage of their numerical superiority arising from the yellow cards issued to the two Welsh players.

55

25 February 2012: Twickenham

19–12: Wales won by 1 try, 1 conversion and 4 penalty goals to 4 penalty goals

Wales: L. Halfpenny; A. Cuthbert (Blues), J. Davies (Scarlets), J. Roberts (Blues), G. North (Scarlets); M. Phillips (Bayonne), R. Priestland (Scarlets); G. Jenkins (Blues), K. Owens (Scarlets), A. Jones, A.W. Jones, I. Evans (Ospreys), D. Lydiate (Dragons), +S. Warburton (Blues), T. Faletau (Dragons).

Replacements: S. Williams (Scarlets) for Roberts; R. Jones (Ospreys) for A.W. Jones.

England: B. Foden; C. Ashton (Northampton), M. Tuilagi (Leicester), B. Barritt, D. Strettle; O. Farrell (Saracens), L. Dickson (Northampton); A. Corbisiero (London Irish), D. Hartley (Northampton), D. Cole (Leicester), M. Botha (Saracens), G. Parling, T. Croft (Leicester), +C. Robshaw (Harlequins), B. Morgan (Scarlets).

Replacements: C. Lawes (Northampton) for Botha; B. Youngs (Leicester) for Dickson; T. Flood (Leicester) for Farrell; M. Stevens (Bath) for Corbisiero; R. Webber (Wasps) for Hartley; M. Brown (Harlequins) for Foden.

This encounter was described by Paul Ackford in *The Telegraph* as 'a tumultuous, exciting, error-ridden, punishing beast of a match'. Its drama lasted until the very last second when the video-referee denied England a try which could have led to a drawn match. However, to all Welsh rugby followers the manner in which Wales had captured the lead for the first time some five minutes earlier with a try by Scott Williams, was even more pulsating.

Both teams experienced periods of superiority, with Wales

starting the match with greater tenacity than their opponents. The hosts, with almost half of their team making their first appearance at Twickenham, seemed to suffer once again from a rather cumbersome approach which often led to their yielding possession, with the industrious Warburton supreme in the tackle area. Wales, on the other hand, continually put England under pressure with powerful drives, including one which saw North almost evade a despairing last-ditch tackle by Strettle and which somehow prevented the Welshman from scoring.

However, after some 20 minutes, the home team gradually took control and a series of sweeping attacks saw Farrell put them ahead with a penalty goal after the opposition centres had strayed off-side in midfield. Within a minute Halfpenny had kicked a penalty goal to bring the teams level. Two further penalty goals by Farrell and one by Priestland saw two evenly-matched teams, after a ferocious and intense first half, retiring with England leading by 9–6.

After four minutes of the second-half they went further ahead when Priestland was penalised for straying off-side while endeavouring to defend his line and tackle Corbisiero following a charge by Botha. As a result the outside-half was given a yellow card and his opposite number kicked the resultant penalty goal. Wales, despite their being a man short, hit back strongly and eight minutes later Halfpenny kicked a penalty goal to make it 12–9. Territorially England at this stage were having the better of the encounter, yet were not able to capitalise on their advantage in that respect. A handling offence in the ruck by Stevens allowed Halfpenny to kick his team level after 71 minutes.

In a frenetically nervous climax, Wales were finishing strongly and with four minutes remaining Scott Williams produced a piece of magic to score the only try of the game. When Halfpenny, running from deep, was collared and turned over, England moved the ball from the left along the line to Lawes who tried to charge through the middle. The vigilant Scott Williams ripped the ball from his grasp near the halfway

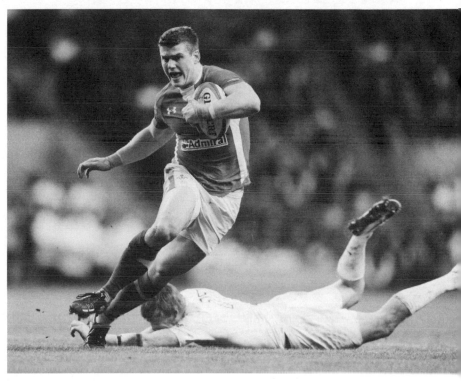

Scott Williams scoring the game's only try with just minutes to go
© Getty Images

and having progressed almost to the home team's ten-metre line, kicked up-field into unguarded territory. With seven English defenders converging on him from all directions, a favourable bounce saw Williams, having gathered the ball some 15 metres out, surge for the line and dive over near the posts for a dramatic try which Halfpenny duly converted.

England weren't finished however, and with little time remaining a penalty took them within metres of the Wales's line on the left-hand side of the field. Following an unsuccessful drive by Parling, the ball was moved quickly to Strettle, in space out on the right wing. In the final seconds of the game, as he endeavoured to crash over in the corner, he was floored by a magnificent tackle from Halfpenny and crucially held up on the line by Davies as the winger tried to get the ball down. The decision as to whether a try had been scored was referred to the video referee who decreed, after a lengthy period of deliberation, that the evidence was too inconclusive to enable him to award a try and that the referee should blow the final whistle.

According to Sam Warburton, their captain, Wales had not played well. Yet, in capturing their 20th Triple Crown with this victory, they had won at Twickenham for only the third time in 24 years.

56

16 March 2013: Millennium Stadium

30–3: Wales won by 2 tries, 1 conversion, 5 penalty goals and 1 drop goal to 1 penalty goal

Wales: L. Halfpenny; A. Cuthbert (Blues), J. Davies (Scarlets), J. Roberts (Blues), G. North (Scarlets); D. Biggar (Ospreys), M. Phillips (Bayonne); +G. Jenkins (Blues), R. Hibbard, A. Jones, A.W. Jones, I. Evans (Ospreys), S. Warburton (Blues), J. Tipuric (Ospreys), T. Faletau (Dragons).

Replacements: K. Owens (Scarlets) for Hibbard; P. James (Bath) for Jenkins; A. Coombs (Dragons) for Evans; A. Shingler (Scarlets) for Roberts; J. Hook (Ospreys) for Biggar; L. Williams (Blues) for Phillips; S. Williams (Scarlets) for Warburton.

England: A. Goode (Saracens); C. Ashton (Northampton), M. Tuilagi (Leicester), B. Barritt (Saracens), M. Brown (Harlequins); O. Farrell (Saracens), B. Youngs (Leicester); J. Marler (Harlequins), T. Youngs (Leicester), D. Cole (Leicester), J. Launchbury (Wasps), G. Parling, T. Croft (Leicester), +C. Robshaw (Harlequins), T. Wood (Northampton).

Replacements: M. Vunipola (Saracens) for Marler; D. Hartley (Northampton) for T. Youngs; C. Lawes (Northampton) for Launchbury; B. Twelvetrees (Gloucester) for Goode; D. Care (Harlequins) for B. Youngs; T. Flood (Leicester) for Farrell; D. Wilson (Bath) for Cole; J. Haskell (Wasps) for Wood.

This was one of the most comprehensive of Welsh victories made all the more palatable for the home supporters by the fact that the much vaunted and hyped opposition were going for the Grand Slam. However, Wales would become Champions if they were to beat England by more than seven points, although, notwithstanding their more recent run of form, they had lost their previous five matches at the Millennium Stadium, including a resounding defeat at the hands of Ireland in the opening game of the Six Nations competition.

From the outset the contest provided a seemingly electrically charged atmosphere with palpable tension pervading the whole stadium. This appeared to trouble the visitors, who had ten of their team playing there for the first time and from the outset Wales dominated the proceedings. Halfpenny opened the scoring with an early penalty goal, one of many conceded by England, particularly for transgressions in the scrums, which, according to Paul Rees in *The Guardian*, became 'a weapon of mass destruction for the home side'. In fact, after just over a quarter of an hour England had yielded five penalties, which equalled the number they conceded throughout the entire match in their previous game against Italy.

Despite the superiority of the home team, at half-time they were ahead by just three penalty goals from Halfpenny to one by Farrell and such a slender margin was the cause of some apprehension among many of their supporters. However, Wales continued to dominate in the second half, as reflected by the fact that their next score, another penalty goal by Halfpenny, was the culmination of their going through 23 phases in the vicinity of the England line.

Surprisingly, perhaps, 55 minutes had elapsed before Wales succeeded in crossing for a try. Following a turn-over achieved by Ken Owens near the halfway line, the ball was moved swiftly by Tupuric (who was awarded the accolade of 'Man of the Match' at the end of the game) via Phillips and Davies to Cuthbert on the right wing who rounded Brown to dive over in the corner. Biggar added a drop goal after 64 minutes before a second try followed for Cuthbert. Following an initial surge by Falletau on his 22-metre line, Warburton stormed through midfield on a 40-metre run. Swift hands saw Tipuric cleverly drawing the England cover defence to release the Cardiff winger who raced

Alex Cuthbert crosses for his second try
© Getty Images

over the line. The try was converted by Biggar, who also added a penalty goal to close the scoring at 30–3.

The visitors could hardly dispute the validity of the scoreline. They had been completely outplayed, particularly in the set pieces. Wales had secured twice as much possession as their opponents and had enjoyed a similar territorial advantage. The reactions of Wales coach, Rob Howley: 'better than the 2012 Grand Slam' and Sam Warburton: 'the best moment of my career', were an indication of the significance of such an achievement for Welsh morale. Such pleasure from the victory and the manner in which it was obtained was also matched by the knowledge that the team had won the Championship for a second successive season, a feat last accomplished in 1978 and 1979.

Post-match media headlines, such as 'Carnage at Cardiff', 'England Steamrollered by Wales' and 'England's Bubble Burst' reflected the superiority of the home team. In the words of the *Daily Mail*:

> For Wales… this was a victory for wit and invention, speed of foot and swiftness of mind. It was a triumph decorated by tries and distinguished by merciless pressure, by well-ordered intensity, by decisions boldly taken and bravely executed. It was the rugby of their glorious heritage and it was altogether too much for England.

BIBLIOGRAPHY

Newspapers:
Western Mail, South Wales Evening Post, South Wales Echo, The Observer, The Guardian, The Daily Mail, The Daily Telegraph

Books:
Phil Bennett, *The Autobiography* (Willow, 2004).
Alun Wyn Bevan, *Straeon o'r Strade* (Gomer, 2004).
Alun Wyn Bevan, *Welsh Rugby Captains* (Gomer, 2010).
John Billot, *History of Welsh International Rugby* (Roman Way, 1999).
Rob Cole and Stuart Farmer, *Wales Rugby Miscellany* (Vision Sports, 2008).
Gareth Davies, and Terry Godwin, *Standing Off* (Queen Anne, 1986).
Gerald Davies, *An Autobiography* (Allen & Unwin, 1979).
Jonathan Davies, with Peter Corrigan, *Jonathan* (Stanley Paul, 1989).
Gareth Edwards, *The Golden Years of Welsh Rugby* (Harrap Ltd 1982).
Gareth Edwards, *100 Great Rugby Players* (Macmillan, 1987).
Gareth Edwards, *The Autobiography* (Headline, 2000).
Alan Evans, *Taming the Tourists* (Vertical Edition, 2003).
Howard Evans and Martyn Williams, *Welsh International Matches 1881–1999* (Mainstream, 1999).
Howard Evans, *Welsh International Matches 1881–2011* (Y Lolfa, 2011).
Ieuan Evans, with Peter Jackson, *Bread of Heaven* (Mainstream, 1995).
David Farmer, *The All Whites: the Life and Times of Swansea RFC* (DFPS, 1995).
Scott Gibbs, *Getting Physical* (Ebury Press, 2000).

Terry Godwin, *The International Rugby Championship 1893–1983* (Willow Books, 1984).

John Griffiths, *Rugby's Strangest Matches* (Portico, 2008).

David Hand, *The Five Nations Story* (Tempus Publishing, 2000)

Terry Holmes, *My Life in Rugby* (Macmillan, 1988).

Peter Jackson, *Lions of Wales: A Celebration of Welsh Rugby Legends* (Mainstream, 1998).

Jenkins, Pierce and Auty, *Who's Who of Welsh International Rugby* (Bridge, 1991).

Neil Jenkins, with Paul Rees, *Life at Number 10* (Mainstream, 1998).

Barry John and Paul Abbandonato, *The King* (Mainstream, 1981).

Robert Jones, *Raising the Dragon* (Virgin, 2001).

Steve Lewis, *The Priceless Gift: 125 years of Welsh Rugby Captains* (Mainstream, 2005).

Cliff Morgan, *The Autobiography – Beyond the Fields of Play* (Hodder & Stoughton, 1996).

David Parry-Jones, *Out of the Ruck* (Pelham, 1986).

David Parry-Jones, *Prince Gwyn* (Seren, 1999).

David Parry-Jones, *The Gwilliam Seasons* (Seren, 2003).

David Parry-Jones, *The Dawes Decades* (Seren, 2005).

John Reason, *Victorious Lions* (Rugby Books, 1971).

John Reason, *The Unbeaten Lions* (Rugby Books, 1974).

John Reason, *Lions Down Under* (Rugby Books, 1977).

John Reason, *Backs to the Wall* (Rugby Books, 1980).

John Reason and Carwyn James, *The World of Rugby: A History of RU Football* (BBC, 1979).

Alun Richards, *A Touch of Glory* (Michael Joseph, 1980).

Huw Richards, *A Game for Hooligans* (Mainstream, 2007).

Huw Richards, *The Red and the White* (Aurum Press, 2009).

Huw Richards, Peter Stead and Gareth Williams (eds), *Heart and Soul* (University of Wales Press, 1998).

Huw Richards, Peter Stead and Gareth Williams (eds), *More Heart and Soul* (University of Wales Press, 1999).

Mark Ring, with Delme Parfitt, *Ringmaster* (Mainstream, 2006).

Clive Rowlands and John Evans, *Clive* (Gomer, 2000).

Clive Rowlands and David Farmer, *Giants of Post-War Welsh Rugby* (Malcolm Press, 1990).

David B. Smith and Gareth W. Williams, *Fields of Praise* (University of Wales Press, 1981).

Clem Thomas and Geoffrey Nicholson, *The Crowning Years* (Collins, 1980).

Clem Thomas and Greg Thomas, *125 Years of the British and Irish Lions* (Mainstream, 2013).

J.B.G. Thomas, *Great Contemporary Players* (Stanley Paul, 1963).

J.B.G. Thomas, *The Men in Scarlet* (Pelham, 1972).

J.B.G. Thomas, *The Illustrated History of Welsh Rugby* (Pelham, 1980).

J.B.G. Thomas, *Rugger in the Blood: Fifty Years of Rugby Memoirs* (Pelham, 1985).

David Watkins, with Brian Dobbs, *The David Watkins Story* (Pelham, 1971).

Gareth Williams, *The First Fifteen* (Parthian, 2011).

J.P.R. Williams, *J.P.R: The Autobiography* (Collins, 1979).

Bobby Windsor and Peter Jackson, *The Iron Duke* (Mainstream, 2010).

Clive Woodward, *Winning* (Hodder & Stoughton, 2004).